MICROSOFT PUBLISHER & ACCESS 2024

A Step-by-Step Practical Guide for Beginner and Professional Users

CHARLES SHERER

Printed in the United States of America

TABLE OF CONTENT

INTRODUCTION 9

BOOK ONE: MICROSOFT PUBLISHER 11

CHAPTER ONE 11

STARTING WITH MICROSOFT PUBLISHER..................................11

CREATING A SHORTCUT FOR PUBLISHER 12

THE RIBBON TABS 14

HOME TAB..14

INSERT TAB...15

PAGE DESIGN TAB 16

THE MAILING TAB 16

REVIEW TAB...16

VIEW TAB..17

FILE BACKSTAGE..17

BUILDING A NEW DESIGN...18

CHAPTER TWO 19

GETTING STARTED WITH A NEW PUBLICATION.........................19

PUBLICATION SIZE 19

ORIENTATION...19

MARGINS 19

OPEN A NEW PUBLICATION..20

THE MAIN WORKSPACE 21

WORKING WITH GUIDES..22

BASIC ELEMENT 23

ADDING A TEXT BOX 24

CREATING TEXT..24

FORMATTING TEXT 25

SPECIFYING FONT 25

ADJUSTING FONT SIZE..26

CHANGING TEXT COLOR 28

SPECIFYING TEXT ALIGNMENT...28

CHANGE CASE 29

EXPLORING TYPOGRAPHY FEATURES...30

ADDING DROP CAP FEATURES 31

STYLISTIC SETS 32

LIGATURES 33

TEXT EFFECTS 34

Shadows..35
Text Outline..35
WordArt styles...36
Formatting Text Boxes..38
Changing Background Color..38
Borders..38
Shadows..39
Styles..40
Altering Text Boxes..40
Repositioning Text Box..40
Reshaping Text Box..41
Rotating Text Box..41
Text Direction..42
Text Autofit..43
Text Box Margins..44
Alignment..45
Joining Text Boxes..46

CHAPTER THREE...48

GETTING STARTED WITH TABLES..48

Resizing Table..49
Moving Table..49
Formatting Your Tables..50
Adding a Column..51
Inserting a Row..51
Resizing Rows & Columns..52
Merge cells..53
Align Cell Text..54
Adding Cell Border..56
Changing Cell Color..57
Text Direction..59

CHAPTER FOUR...60

WORKING GRAPHICS...60

Adding images..60
Image from Google..62
Adding clipart..64
Adding Effects to Images..66
Add a Caption..68
Cropping Images..69

CROP TO SHAPE 71

ADJUSTING YOUR IMAGES 74

WRAPPING TEXT AROUND IMAGES 75

WRAPPING POINTS 76

ADDING SHAPES TO YOUR PUBLICATION 78

ALTERING SHAPES 79

CHANGING THE COLOR 79

CHANGING THE BORDER 80

ADDING A SHADOW 81

OBJECTS ALIGNMENT 83

OBJECTS DISTRIBUTION 84

GROUPING OBJECTS 86

POSITIONING OBJECT LAYERS 87

PAGE PARTS 87

ADDING BORDERS AND ACCENTS 91

INSERTING CALENDARS INTO YOUR PUBLISHER 92

CREATING OF ADVERTISEMENTS 94

ADDING WORDART 96

CHAPTER FIVE **102**

CREATING MAIL MERGE **102**

CREATING A MAIL MARGE ENVELOPES 102

CREATING MAIL MERGE INVITATION 108

USING PRE-DESIGNED TEMPLATES 113

FINDING A PRE-DESIGNED TEMPLATE 113

MAKING YOUR TEMPLATE 115

CHAPTER SIX **117**

MANAGING PUBLICATION **117**

SAVING YOUR PUBLICATION AS A DIFFERENT FORMAT 119

OPENING SAVED DOCUMENTS 122

USING PAGE SETUP 124

CREATING BOOKLETS 127

USING PAGE MASTERS 130

EDITING MASTER PAGES 130

CREATING MASTER PAGES 132

APPLYING MASTER 134

INSERTING GUIDES 134

CHAPTER SEVEN **138**

PUBLISHING YOUR WORK **138**

Printing Your Documents...138

Printing as Booklet 140

Exporting Your Work as a PDF 143

Share a File..145

BOOK TWO: MICROSOFT ACCESS..**147**

CHAPTER ONE **147**

GETTING STARTED WITH ACCESS **147**

Understanding Database 148

Database tables for storing information......................................149

Generating a Database File 152

Obtaining the assistance of a template 156

Moving Around the Navigation Pane..157

Designing a database 159

Determining what information you want 159

Separating information into diverse database tables 160

Choosing fields for database tables 162

Deciding on a primary key field for each database table 163

Mapping the relationships between tables...................................164

CHAPTER TWO **165**

CONSTRUCTING YOUR DATABASE TABLES **165**

Generating a database table 165

Generating a database table from scratch 166

Importing the database table from another database 169

Obtaining the help of a template 170

Opening and Viewing Tables..171

Entering and Changing Table Fields 173

Everything about data types 176

Designating the primary key field 177

Moving, renaming, and deleting fields..178

CHAPTER THREE **179**

FIELD PROPERTIES FOR MAKING SURE THAT DATA ENTRIES ARE PRECISE **179**

Field Properties settings 180

Creating a lookup data-entry list 183

Creating a drop-down list on your own.......................................184

Getting list items from a database table 185

Indexing for Faster Sorts, Searches, and Queries 186

Indexing a field 186

Indexing created on more than one field 186
Dealing with tables in the Relationships window 188
Falsifying relationships between tables 189
Editing and Deleting table relationships 190

CHAPTER FOUR 191

ENTERING THE DATA 191

Two Ways to Enter Data 191
Entering the Data in Datasheet View 191
Two tricks for entering data quicker 192
Entering the Data in a form 192
Creating a form 193
Entering the data 195
Discovery of a Missing Record 195
Finding and Replacing Data 196

CHAPTER FIVE 198

SORTING AND FILTERING FOR DATA 198

Sorting Records in a Database Table 198
Sorting records 198
Filtering to discover information 198
Diverse ways to filter a database table 199
Unfiltering a database table 199
Filtering by selection 199
Filtering by form 200
Filtering for input 201

CHAPTER SIX 202

QUERYING: THE FUNDAMENTALS 202

Creating a new query 202
Viewing queries in Design and Datasheet views 203
Navigating your way around the Query Design window 204
Selecting which database tables to query 205
Selecting which fields to query 206
Sorting the query outcomes or results 207
MOVING FIELD COLUMNS ON THE QUERY GRID 207
Entering criteria for a query 207
Saving and running a query 208
Six kinds of Queries 209

CHAPTER SEVEN 211

PRESENTING DATA IN A REPORT **211**

    CREATING A REPORT 211

    OPENING AND VIEWING REPORTS 212

    FINE-TUNING A REPORT..213

CONCLUSION **215**

INDEX **216**

INTRODUCTION

Microsoft Publisher is a mighty instrument that can help businesses create newsletters, invitation cards, and other marketing materials. The publisher is a desktop publishing and layout application part of the Microsoft Office suite, it creates and designs professional-looking marketing and communication documents such as posters, business cards, flyers, catalogs, and brochures.

The purpose of Microsoft publishers is to supply users with an instrument for creating professional quality communication and marketing materials, it also offers maximum templates and features that can make it easy to design and create a high-quality document, the publisher is considered an entry-level desktop application and it is directed at home users, schools, and small businesses, the publisher is not used for commercial printing purposes.

The publisher is different from Microsoft Word in such a way that the emphasis is placed on page design and layout rather than text composition and proofreading. You can easily create many different types of publications by making use of a publisher, the publisher also permits you to freely layout your designs on the page using objects like text boxes for headings and body text, and image placeholders for shapes and photographs. Publisher contains diverse pre-design templates, and building blocks that can be used for creating bigger publications called 'page parts'

This book covers publishers in all dimensions, from beginner to expert. I did not brandish my grammatical skills while in this book, therefore readers of all educational levels should be able to understand every page, despite their level of knowledge.

Microsoft Access on the other hand is a database application management that permits you to keep and manage large collections of data and assist you in recovering them back when it is needed. Until there is an introduction of Microsoft Access certain organization needs may not be acquired.

This user guide is primarily prepared to put you on a plane track and pathway in mastering Access, it is a comprehensive practical lesson of total breakthrough from Access tools, this user guide offers you an easy means of learning and a quick understanding of the following Access apparatus and tools:

- Getting started with Access.
- Create a database file that you will use to save the database information.
- Working with the Access Navigation pane.
- Getting started with the construction of the database table.
- Entering fields into each database table.
- Entering data directly into the table or employing the help of a Form.
- Managing tables relationship in the relationship windows for effective database query.
- Working with the Query Design Window.
- Format for entering the correct criteria when querying the database for particular information.
- Creating a specialized report through the query results.
- Refining the appearance of the Report. And a lot more.

BOOK ONE: MICROSOFT PUBLISHER

Chapter One

Starting with Microsoft Publisher

With a publisher, you can easily create many different types of publications. Publisher varies from Microsoft Word in that special importance is placed on page layout design rather than text composition and attestability.

Microsoft Publisher is a desktop publishing Application developed by Microsoft. The publisher is considered an entry-level desktop publishing application and is aimed at home users, schools, and small businesses with in-house printing. Publisher

is not used for commercial printing purposes.

The publisher uses a WYSIWYG interface (what you see is what you get), which simply means, that every single thing you create on the screen appears the same way when printed.

Publisher provides various features and tools to create and edit publications such as posters, banners, flyers, letterheads, greeting cards, and banners. These tools are categorized into tabs in a menu system on the top of the screen called a ribbon.

Publishers permit you to freely sketch your designs on the page using objects such as text boxes for headings and body text, and image placeholders for photographs and shapes.

The publisher also includes building blocks for creating bigger publications named "page part" and pre-designed templates.

proofing tools such as grammar check, and spell checkers permit you to verify your work as you type. Grammar errors are marked in green while the misspelled words are underlined in red. Commonly misspelled phrases or words are corrected by auto-correct features.

Follow the steps itemized below to launch Microsoft Publisher on your PC:

1. Enter "**Publisher**" into the **Search** box at the bottom left of the Window

2. Then click the **'Publisher'** desktop app as slightly shaded beneath.

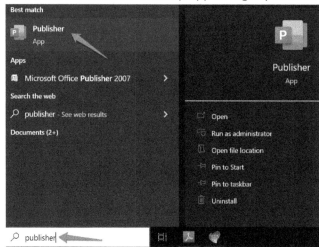

3. (Alternatively), click the **Start** button and click **Publisher** on the available items.

Creating a Shortcut for Publisher

To make it simpler, you can nail the publisher icon on the taskbar. I find this attribute very useful. To do this follow the steps below

1. Right-click on the **Publisher** icon on the taskbar.

2. click "**pin to taskbar**".

In this manner, the publisher will always be on the taskbar anytime you need it.

Once the publisher begins, on the right-hand side you can select a template from the thumbnails by clicking anyone to start.

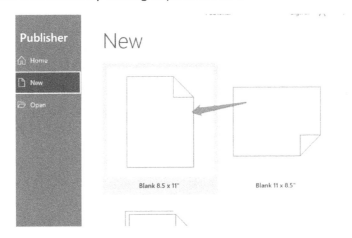

At the left-hand side green pane your most newly saved publications will be shown, let's briefly take a look at the publisher's main screen. Here we can see below, the screen is split into divisions

The Ribbon Tabs

Publisher tools are categorized into tabs called ribbons along the uppermost of the screen, tools are categorized according to their function, and they are as follows.

Home Tab

All tools that as to do with test constructing, such as: changing the fonts and making text bold, and the most common tools for text formatting and alignment.

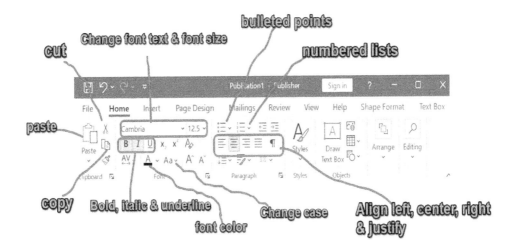

Insert Tab

All tools that as to do with inserting borders, tables, graphics Photos, charts, etc.

You can also insert word Art, graphics, equations, pre-designed ads, page parts, and smart art using the "building blocks" and "illustrations" sections of the ribbon.

You can also include or insert word art, text boxes, and symbols using the text section of the ribbon.

Page Design Tab

The page design ribbon permits you to adjust the margin, page orientation, and size, change templates and set up design guides to help you with the elements on your page.

You can also set up page masters, change the background, and pick or elect pre-designed schemes.

The Mailing Tab

Mailing ribbon permits you to set up mail merges in your publisher document and connect it to a data source in a spreadsheet

Review Tab

You can do some research with the review ribbon, and you can also spell check your document, translate text into order language, and lock up words in the thesaurus.

View Tab

You can change the default view, add rulers, zoom, and navigation with the view ribbon, and also change your open master pages by using the view ribbon.

File Backstage

When you click "File" on the uppermost of your screen on the left-hand side, this will open up what Microsoft refers to as the "Backstage".

Backstage is where you save or open publications, share or export publications, print, as well as options, preference settings, and a Microsoft account.

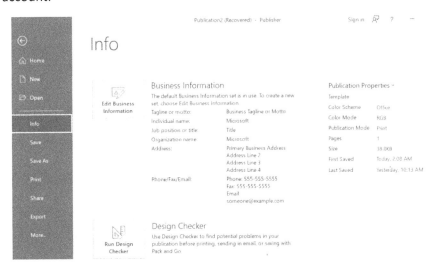

You can also change publication preferences, Microsoft Account Settings, login, and initiate your Microsoft Office.

Building A New Design

You can effortlessly make various designs with Microsoft Publisher, you can design them from scrape, or one of the many different patterns or frameworks included with the application.

Chapter Two

Getting Started with a New Publication

You will need to make a little choice about a certain aspect, such as paper type, size, and page layout before you make a new publication. Some of the choices you have to make about your publication include page layout. Making a publication from a template takes care of most of the following for you.

Publication Size

Some publications, like flyers, can be small, A6 or A5. Order publications include such posters that are a lot bigger, A1 or A3.

Preset Page Sizes

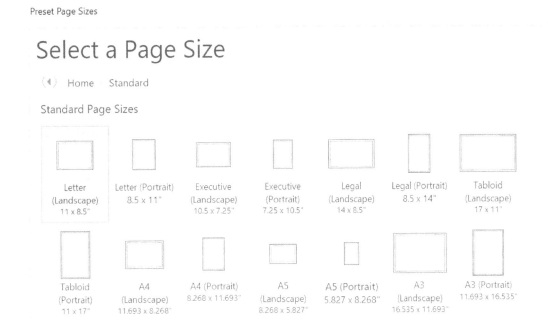

Orientation

Portrait or landscape. various flyers are portrait, likewise most posters. Greetings cards can also be both portrait and landscape orientation.

Margins

The areas of blank space around the top, bottom, right, and left edges of a printed publication are called **"margins"**.

Open a new publication

You will be able to pick a template, to begin with, or create a blank publication when you open Publishers. For this demo pick "blank A4 (portrait)".

If you are running your publisher right now click "File" on the uppermost screen at the left-hand side then select "New" Then you will surely land on the publisher's main work area, and immediately you will pick a New template.

Here we can start creating our publication.

The Main Workspace

You will see your page navigation pane on the left-hand side. Here, you can see the number of pages in your navigation pane. You need to click on the page thumbnails in the navigation pane to jump to that page.

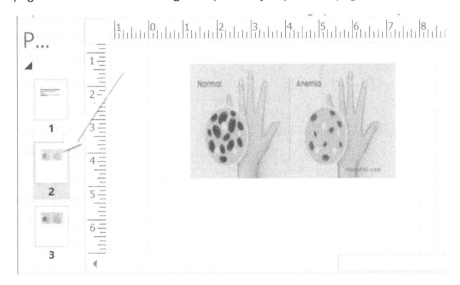

You will see three sets of values at the base (the underside or bottom) of the screen. The first will show you the page number you are on, click to open and close the page navigation pane. The second set will show you the position of the top and left corners of an object on your page. And therefore the object selected below is 12.75cm down from the and 4.92cm from the left edge of the page. The last set of numbers shows the size of the selected object.

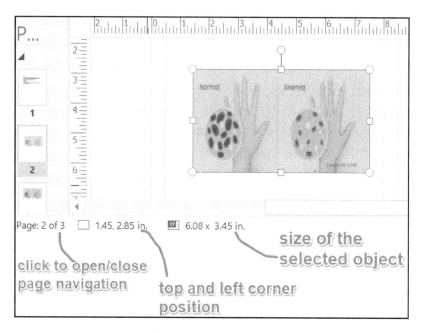

On the bottom right, you will notice the page zoom and page view controls

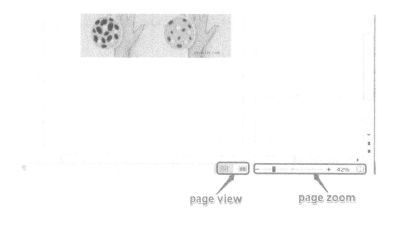

WORKING WITH GUIDES

To create guidelines to help you align the elements on your design, click either the vertical or horizontal ruler, then you can now drag your mouse pointer to the position on your page.

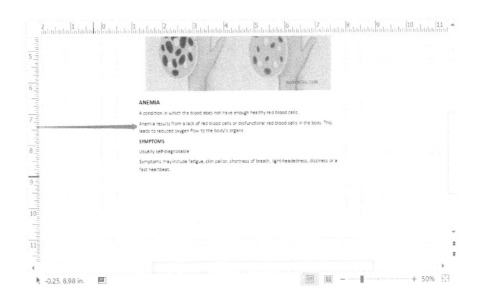

Basic Element

Publisher documents are designed using some of these basic elements such as text box and image placeholder.

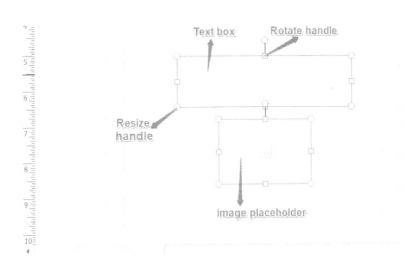

You can add text boxes to your design to entail the text and place it separately. You can do the same thing with image placeholders. These are used to place images in your design. You can also call these placeholders"

Frames". When you click on a placeholder or frame, small circles will display around the edge and they are called handles. You can click and drag on the handles to rescale your image placeholder or text box, you can also add charts, tables, and shapes to your designs.

Adding a Text Box

To add certain text to your design, the first thing you have to do is to add a text box, and for you to add a text box you need to go to the home ribbon

And select "draw text box".

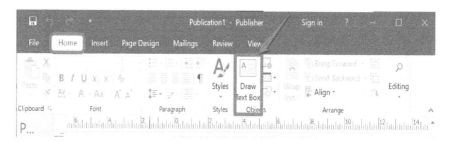

Click and drag the text box on your page

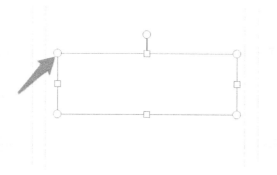

Creating Text

You can type in some text, once you have inserted a text box.

Formatting Text

You can format your text within your text box by using the basic formatting tools on the home ribbon.

Specifying Font

Follow these steps to change the font

1. Highlight the text you want to change.

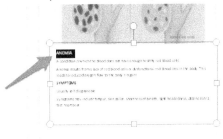

2. Click on the font from the home ribbon, then Select the font you want, from the drop-down box.

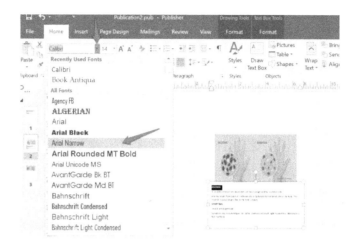

Adjusting Font Size

The text you want to change needs to be highlighted.

Select the font size from the home ribbon, then from the drop-down select the size you want.

Bold, italic, underlined

Highlight the text you want to change.

Click the bold icon on the top left of the home ribbon. Do the same for Italic and underlined text.

Changing Text Color

Highlight the text you want to change.

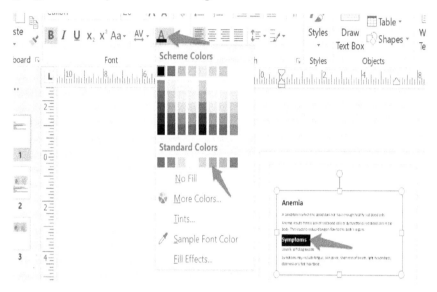

Select the font color icon from the home ribbon. Select a color from the drop-down list.

Specifying Text Alignment

Inside your text box, you can align text to the right, left, or center. You can also completely justify text so a text block is aligned to both the right and left of the text box.

For you to do this, select the text you want to align.

Select a paragraph alignment icon, from the home ribbon.

Change Case

You can speedily change the case of the text to sentence case, UPPERCASE, or lowercase. To do this select your text.

Select the case change icon from the home tab.

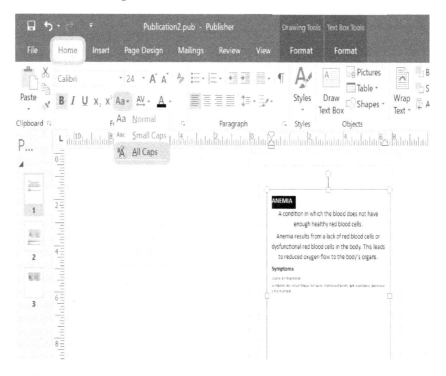

Exploring Typography Features

The publisher consists of diverse typography features to help you format your text. It's essential to note that these effects only work with certain fonts, such as Zapfino, Garamond, Cambria, and Gabriola.

Adding Drop Cap Features

A drop cap expands the first letter of the selected text and is frequently used at the block of text or the start of the chapter. To do this, you need to click on the paragraph you want to drop the cap.

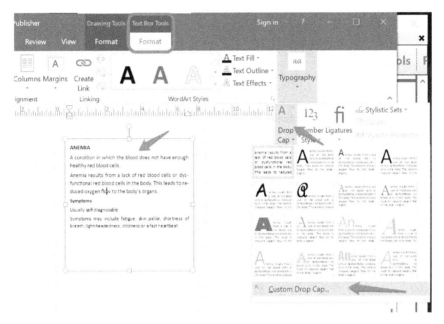

From the "text box tools" format ribbon, choose "drop cap". now you can click "custom drop cap" or select a pre-set style from the options.

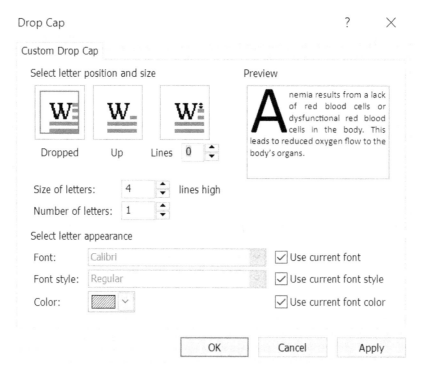

Change the size of letters to fit your drop cap into the paragraph, you can also change the color and font. Click on 'apply' when you are through.

Stylistic sets

These sets let you choose between diverse styles for your fonts, usually in the form of flourishes or exaggerated serifs. Highlight the letter, then from the 'text box tools' format ribbon select 'stylistic sets'

Now select an option from the drop-down box.

At the same time, you can make use of a stylistic set of words. It is also useful for creating fancy headings and titles.

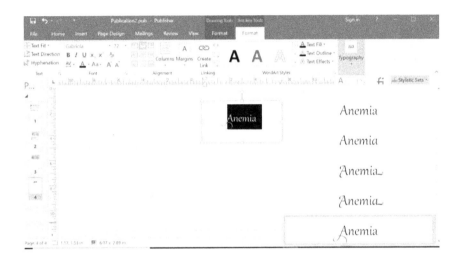

Ligatures

Ligatures attach certain combinations of letters to make them very simple to read. There are many diverse ligatures. *ff, ct, fi sp, st, ffi, th* being the most common.

The ligature can be turned on from the "text box tools" format ribbon. Select the character, then select "ligature".

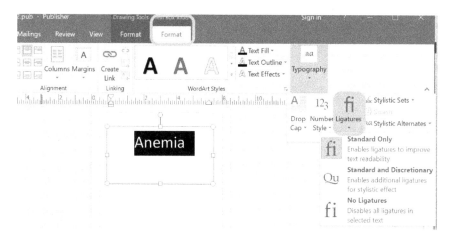

Stylistic Alternatives

This offers diverse versions of certain letters. You will locate these alternatives on the "text box tools" format ribbon. Select the character, then select "stylistic Alternative".

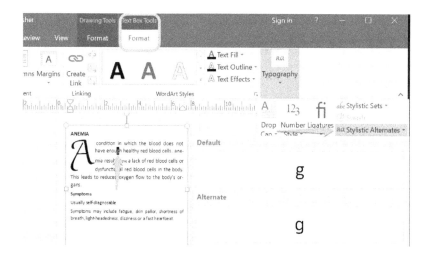

Text Effects

You can add reflections, glow, bevel, and shadows to your text, as well as change the style and add fill color and outline.

Shadows

If you want to add shadow, select the text you would like to use, then from the 'text box tools' format tab, then select 'text effects'.

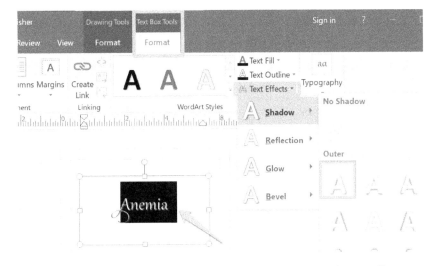

Select an effect from the list. Then you can also add a glow, reflection, or bevel effects from here.

Text Outline

To add an outline, you will have to select the text you want to use, then from the 'text tools' format tab, select 'text outline.

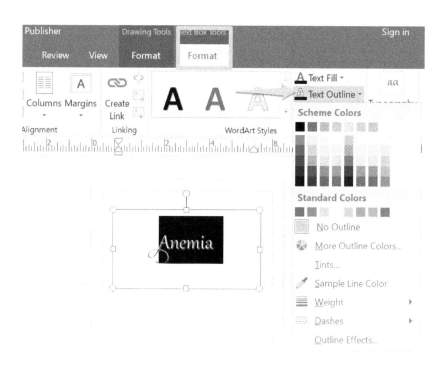

WordArt styles

To use Wordart style, select the text you would like to use, then from the 'text box tools' format tab, select a style from the Wordart.

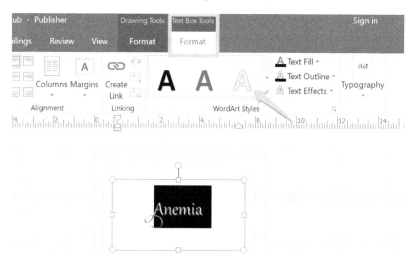

To view more styles, Click the small down arrow nearby the WordArt styles.

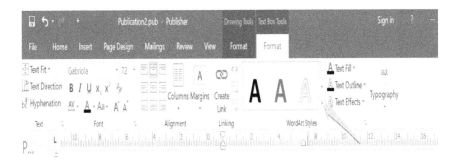

You will see a plentiful list of options.

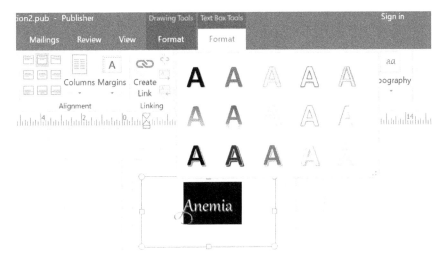

choose a style. You can choose from several predetermined styles.

Formatting Text Boxes

You can include bevels, shadows, and reflections in your text boxes, you can apply another style, and also add an outline and fill color.

Changing Background Color

You will select the text box, then under the 'drawing tools' select the 'format' ribbon. Select 'shape fill'.

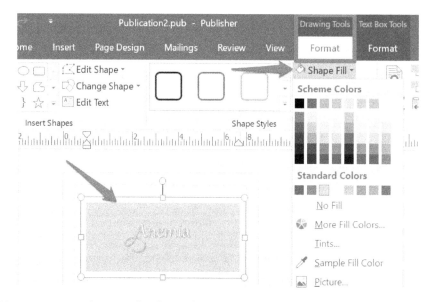

You can now select a color from the drop-down list.

Borders

Select the text box, then below the 'drawing tools' select the 'format' ribbon. Select 'shape outline'.

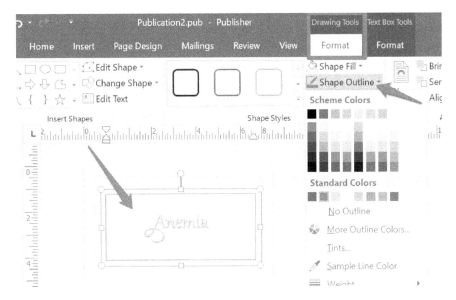

Select a color from the drop-down list.

Shadows

Select the text box, then below the 'drawing tools' select the 'format' ribbon. Then select 'shape effects'.

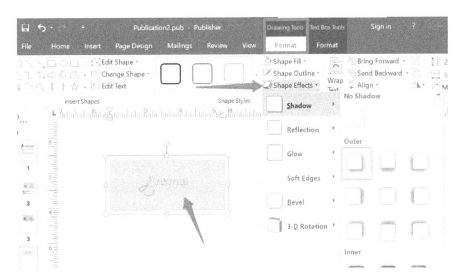

Move down to 'shadows', then select an effect from the slideout.

Styles

There are diverse predetermined styles you can use to beautify your text boxes. To use them:

1) select the text box, and choose the 'Drawing tool format' tab.
2) Click the little arrow nearby the shape styles to open the panel.

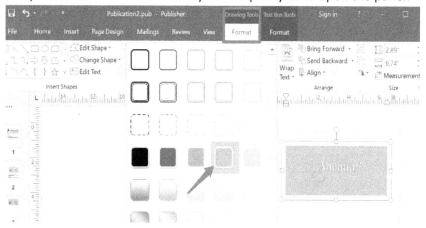

Select a style.

Altering Text Boxes

You can resize, move, and rotate the text boxes, as well as change the alignment, text direction, and margins.

Repositioning Text Box

Click on the text box's border to move a text box. Then drag the box to its newest location.

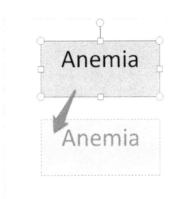

Reshaping Text Box

For you to resize a text box, click and drag one out of the resize handles till the box is the desired size.

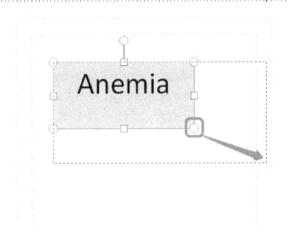

Rotating Text Box

To rotate a text box, click and drag the rotate handle on the topmost central of the box. Then drag your mouse to the left or right to adjust the rotation.

Text Direction

The direction of the text in a text box can be changed. To rotate your text, select the text box, then from the 'text box tools' format ribbon, click 'text direction'.

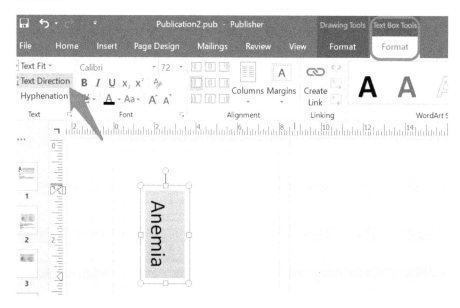

Text Autofit

You can naturally size and fit text inside your text boxes. To do this, select the text box you want to change, then from the format tab under 'text box tools', choose 'text fit'.

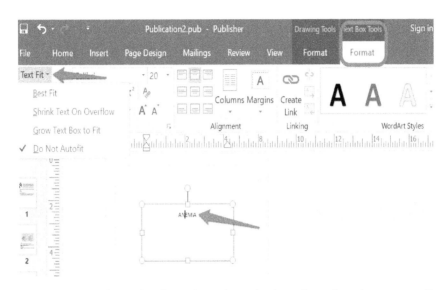

Select an option from the drop-down list. The best fit makes the text smaller or bigger to fit the text box.

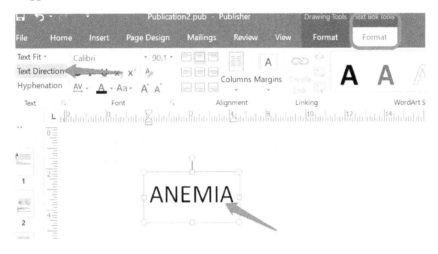

Shrink text on overflow naturally shrinks the text as you type to fill the size of the text box. Grow text box to fit naturally increases the size of the text box according to the text's size.

Text Box Margins

You can adjust the margins inside the text box. The margin is the gap between the edge of the text box and the text. Click the text box, to adjust the text margin.

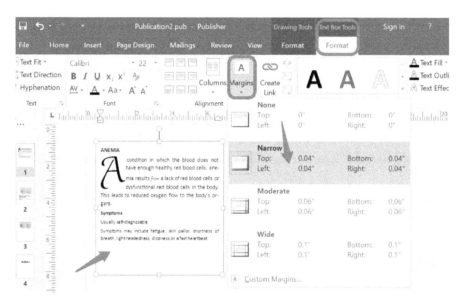

From the 'text box tools' format ribbon, select 'margins'. You can also select one out of the four presents, or click 'custom margins'.

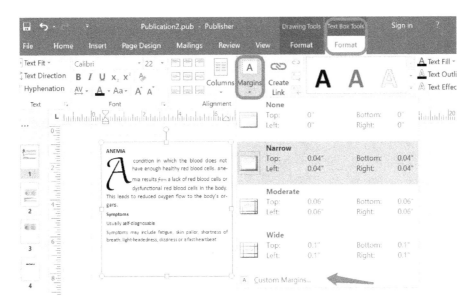

From here, you can independently adjust each of the four margins.

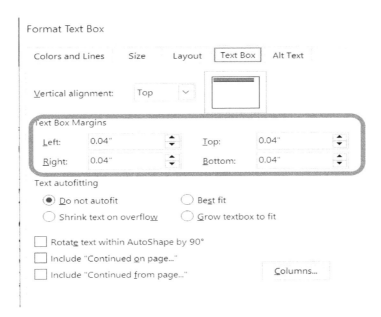

Alignment

You can align your text within your text box. You can align to the right, left, middle, top, bottom, or middle. To do this, click the text box, then from the 'text box tools' format ribbon, from the alignment section on the ribbon, select the alignment icon.

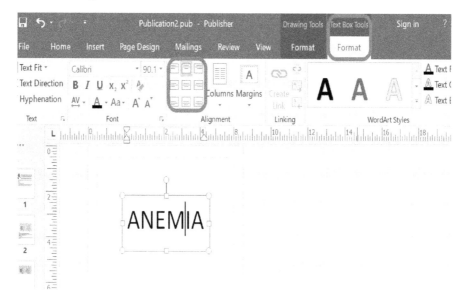

Joining Text Boxes

As you work with the text boxes, You might discover that a text box isn't big enough to entail all of the tests you want to incorporate. You can link the boxes when you run out of room for text. Text will overflow or continue from one text box to the next once two or more text boxes are linked. Select your 'text box tools' format ribbon, and click 'create a link'.

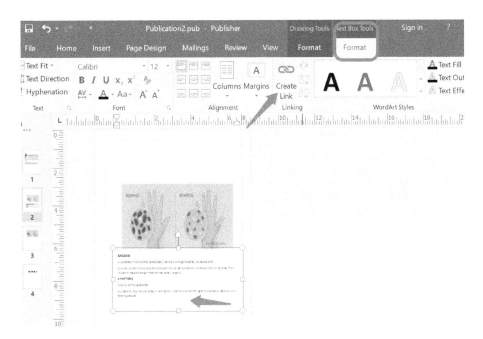

The pointer of your mouse will turn into a 'link icon'. Click the position on your page where you like to link to.

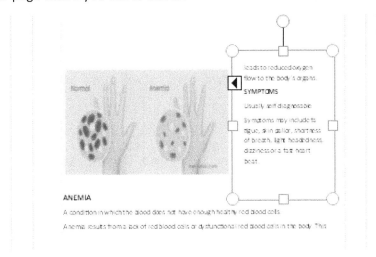

A new test box will come over. As you type your text, the text will overflow onto the order text box.

Chapter Three

Getting Started with Tables

We have added a few more texts about the percentage of anemia in the world to our document. Right now we will add a table to illustrate our text. Go to your insert ribbon and select the table to insert a table.

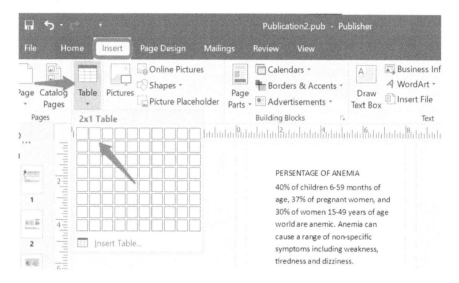

In the grid that comes over highlight the number of rows and columns you need. For this table, 1 row and 2 columns. This will add a table with 1 row and 2 columns to your document.

Drag the table into position and input your data. To navigate within cells on the table press the tab key. When you reach the end of the row, pressing the tab will add a new row.

PERCENTAGE OF ANEMIA

40% of children 6-59 months of age, 37% of pregnant women, and 30% of women 15-49 years of age world are anemic. Anemia can cause a range of non-specific symptoms including weakness, tiredness and dizziness.

Category	Percentage
Children 6-59 months of age	40%
Pregnant women	37%
Women 15-49	30%

Resizing Table

click and drag one of the corners of the grey borders To resize a table.

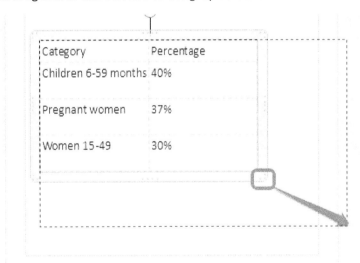

Moving Table

To move your table, just click anywhere on the table, then click and drag the border.

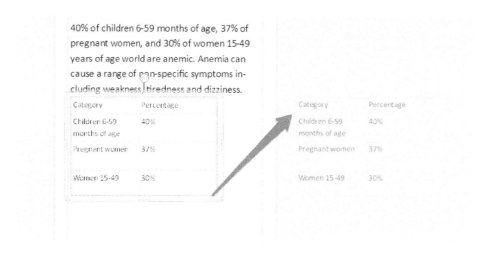

40% of children 6-59 months of age, 37% of pregnant women, and 30% of women 15-49 years of age world are anemic. Anemia can cause a range of non-specific symptoms including weakness, tiredness and dizziness.

Category	Percentage
Children 6-59 months of age	40%
Pregnant women	37%
Women 15-49	30%

Category	Percentage
Children 6-59 months of age	40%
Pregnant women	37%
Women 15-49	30%

Formatting Your Tables

Immediately you click on the table in your document, two new ribbons will come over below 'table tools': design and layout. The design ribbon will permit you to select pre-set designs for your tables, such as borders, color, column, and row shading. At the center of your design ribbon, you will discover a list of designs. Click on the small arrow at the bottom right of the 'tables styles' panel to open it up.

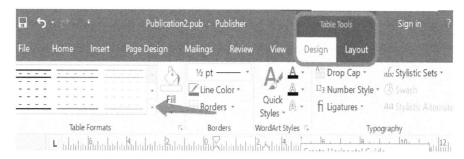

For this table, I will choose one with shaded rows and blue headings.

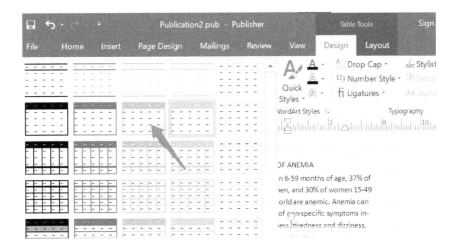

Adding a Column

You can add a column to the right-hand side of your table. To do this, click inside the end column

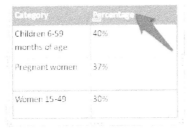

Select the layout ribbon under 'table tools', and select 'insert right'.

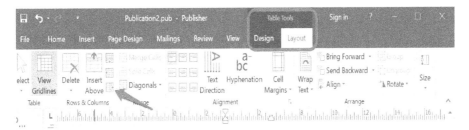

Inserting a Row

to insert a row, click on the row where you want to insert it. I want to add a row between pregnant women and women 15-49. So click on women 15-49, as shown below.

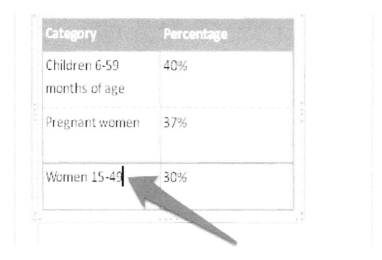

Click on the layout ribbon from the table tools section.

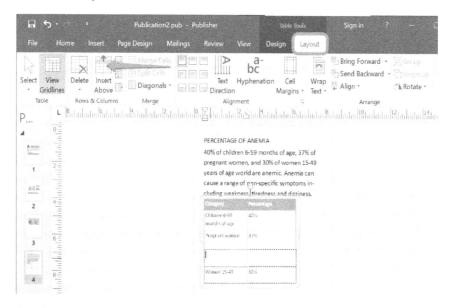

Click 'insert above'. This will input a row above the one chosen earlier.

Resizing Rows & Columns

To resize the row and column you can do that by clicking and dragging the row and column splitting line to the size you want.

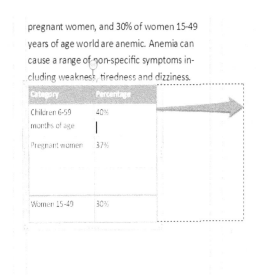

pregnant women, and 30% of women 15-49 years of age world are anemic. Anemia can cause a range of non-specific symptoms including weakness, tiredness and dizziness.

Category	Percentage
Children 6-59 months of age	40%
Pregnant women	37%
Women 15-49	30%

Merge cells

You can merge cells by following the steps below:

1. Select and highlight the cells you want to merge.
2. Then select 'merge cells' from the ribbon in the table tools section.

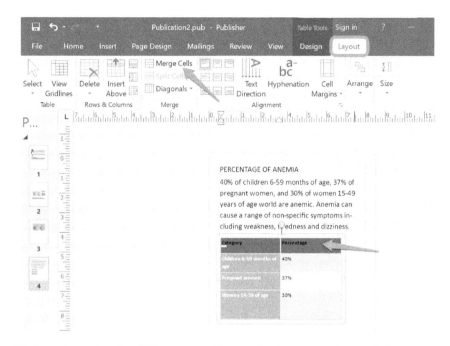

All the selected cells will be merged into a single one as shown below.

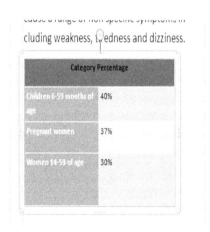

Align Cell Text

For you to be able to change the text alignment in the cells of the table, the first thing is to select the cells you want to align. Click and drag.

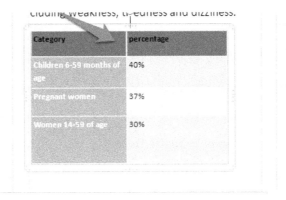

Then select the layout ribbon in the table tools section, as shown under.

From the alignment section, make use of the nine boxes to select the text alignment you want to assign to the cells.

Below is a quick guide to what the nine diverse alignments look like. In the diagram beneath, note where every single box on the left puts the text in the cells in the example on the right.

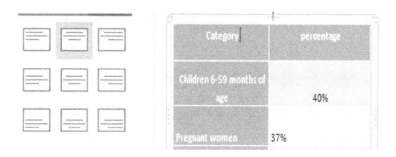

For example, select the center box to align the cells to the center of the cell.

Adding Cell Border

pick the cells you want to add a border to.

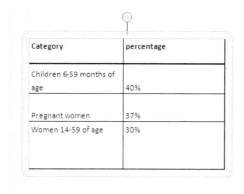

Click the 'table tools' design tab. Choose a line thickness

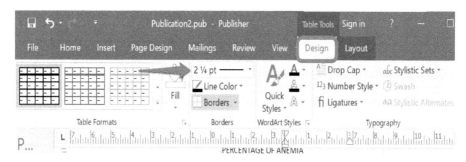

choose a line color

56

Click on the 'borders'. From the drop-down list, choose where on your selection you want the borders to come into sight.

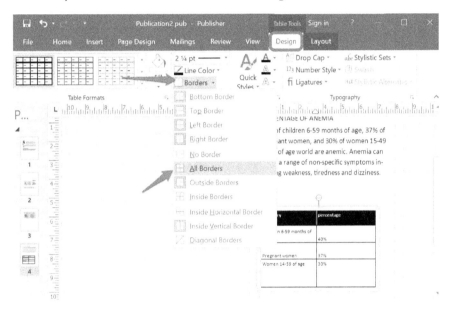

Changing Cell Color

choose the cell or cells you want to change color

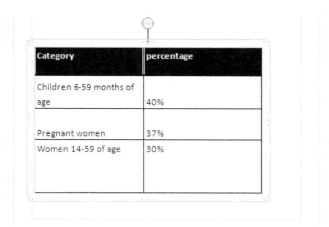

Category	percentage
Children 6-59 months of age	40%
Pregnant women	37%
Women 14-59 of age	30%

choose the 'table tools' design tab.

Click on the fill. Then choose a color from the pallet.

Text Direction

You can organize the text vertically, this works for the headings most of the time

To do this, select the heading rows in your table.

Then click 'text direction' from the layout ribbon.

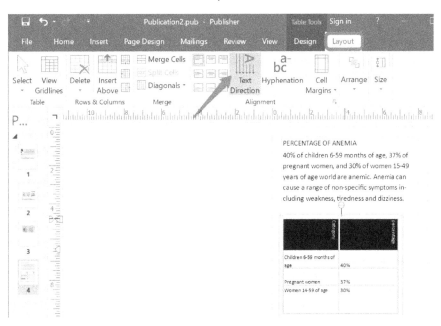

Chapter Four

Working Graphics

In this section, we will be looking at adding shapes, images, and other tools to add some color to our publication.

Adding images

Adding images to your document is simple. There are two ways you can add images to your document, your pictures and photos stored on your OneDrive or computer.

Go to your 'insert ribbon' and click on 'pictures'.

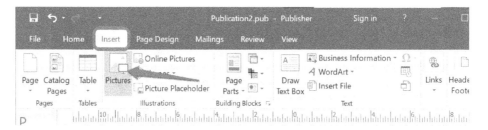

Select the picture or photo you would like to use from the dialog box that appears. Click Insert.

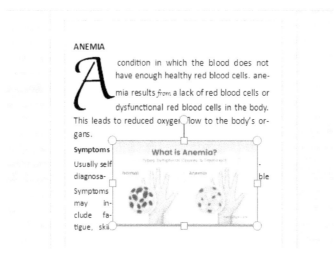

This will import your photo into your document.

You may need to resize the photo, once inserted into the publisher, as sometimes they can come in a bit large. To do this click on the photo or image, you will notice small handles appear on each corner of the image. These are called resize handles. They can be used by clicking and dragging a corner towards the middle of the image to make it smaller as shown below. Hold down the shift key as you resize the image to prevent it from being deformed.

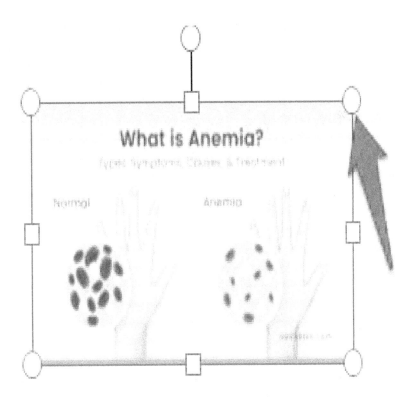

Click and drag the photo into place on your document.

ANEMIA

A condition in which the blood does not have enough healthy red blood cells. anemia results *from* a lack of red blood cells or dysfunctional red blood cells in the body. This leads to reduced oxygen flow to the body's organs.

Symptoms

Usually self-diagnosable

Symptoms may include fatigue, skin pallor, shortness of breath, light-headedness, dizziness or a fast heartbeat

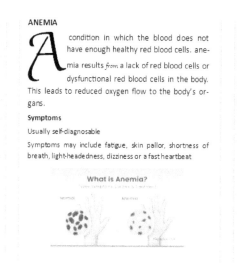

Image from Google

You can search for images on Google. When you download an image, make sure you save it in your pictures folder. Open your web browser and make a Google search, then select 'images'.

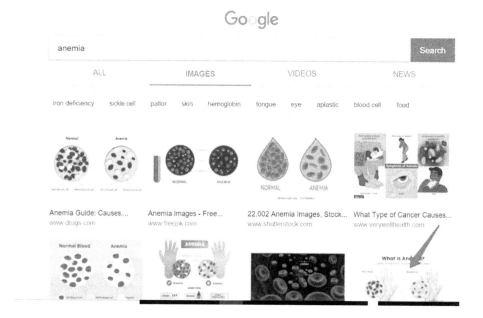

Click the image thumbnail in the search results to see the full-size image. Right-click the image, then choose 'save image as' from the popup menu.

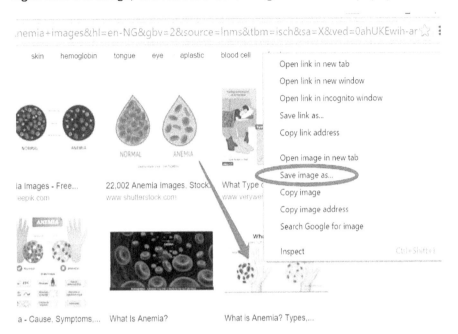

From the dialog box that comes into sight, save the picture into your 'picture folder' either on your PC or OneDrive folder.

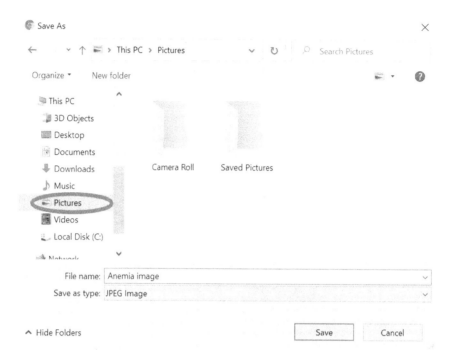

Immediately your image is saved into your pictures folder, you can import them into your Publisher document using the same process at the beginning of the chapter.

Adding clipart

To proceed with our document, I will be adding a new section called **Worldwide Percentage of Anemia** and I need some clipart to illustrate this.

To add a clipart image, visit your insert ribbon and click 'online pictures'.

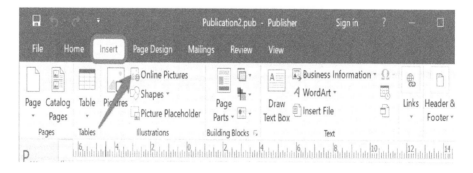

Then type in what you are looking for in the dialog box, as shown below. In this example, enter the search term 'Anemia'

Note this, you will need an internet connection for you to be able to get what you are searching for.

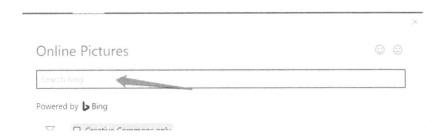

In the search results, choose the image you want then click Insert.

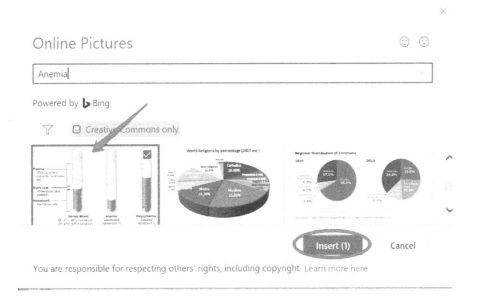

You might need to rescale and position the image. Hold down the shift key as you rescale the image to stop it from being deformed.

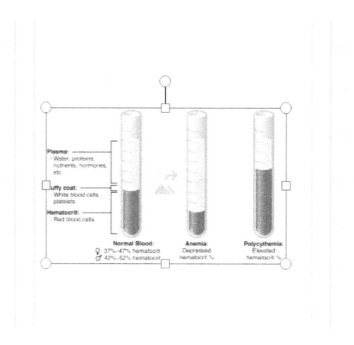

Adding Effects to Images

To add effects to your images, such as borders and shadows, click on your image, and select the 'Pictures tools' format tab. In this example, click on the anemia image.

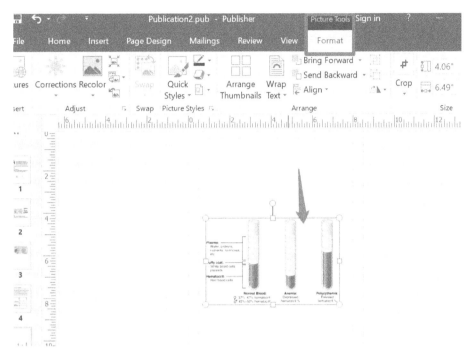

I would like to create a nice reflection style for the image. For me to do this, I will click on 'picture effects', then proceed to 'reflection'. Select a variation as shown below.

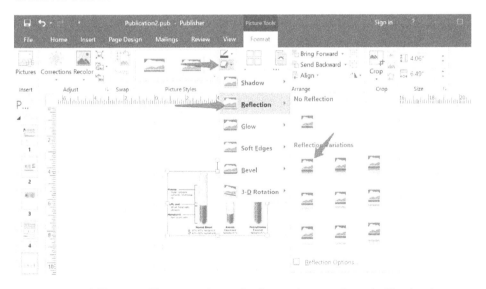

You can try different effects, such as **shadow, glow, or bevel.** Check what effect they have…

Add a Caption

You need to click the image you want to add the caption to, then from the 'picture tools' format ribbon select 'caption'. Then from the drop-down menu, select a caption style.

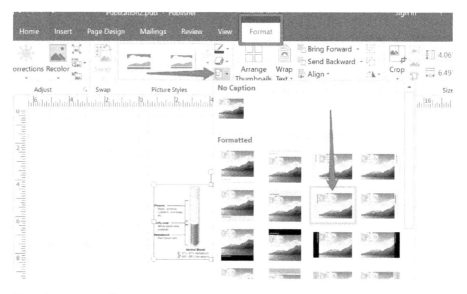

Type in your caption...

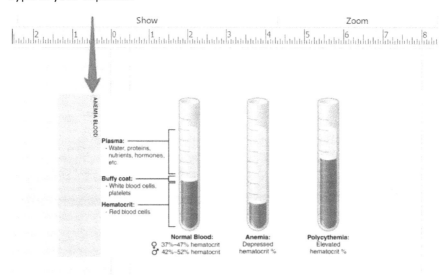

Cropping Images

For instance, if you import an image into your document, and you discover it has an unwanted portion or you want to focus on one particular area of the picture, you can crop the image

First, import an image from your pictures library into your document.

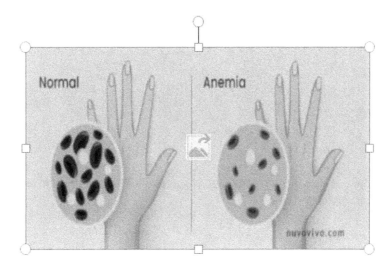

To crop, click on the image, then click the 'picture tools' format tab. From the format ribbon, click the crop icon.

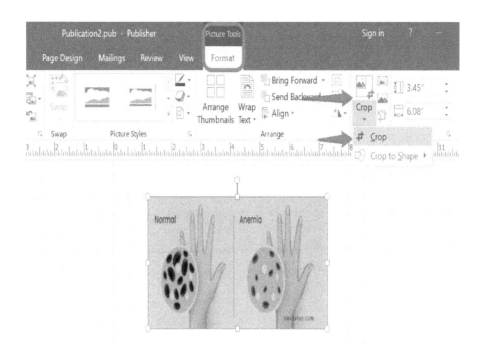

If you take a look around your image, you will see crop handles around the edges, as displayed below.

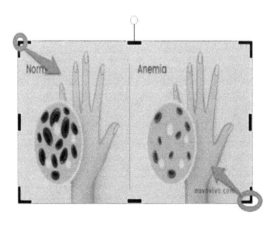

Click and drag these handles around the area of the image you want. E.g, I will like to keep Anemia in the image.

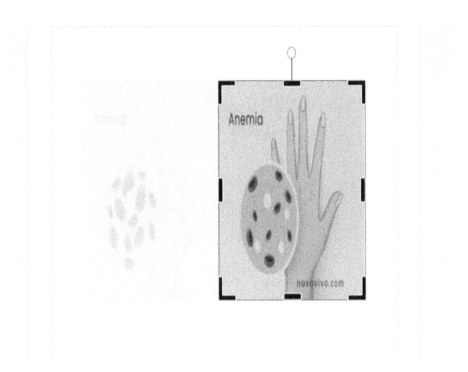

Click anywhere on your document to finish, the light grey bits will be cut off to leave the bit of the image inside the crop square.

Crop to shape

For you to crop an image to fit within a shape. The first thing you need to do is to insert an image from your pictures library into your document.

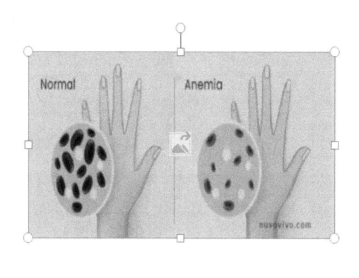

To do this follow the steps below:

1. Click on the image.
2. Then click on the 'picture tools' format tab.
3. Click on the down arrow beneath the crop icon.
4. Select 'crop to shape' From the drop-down list

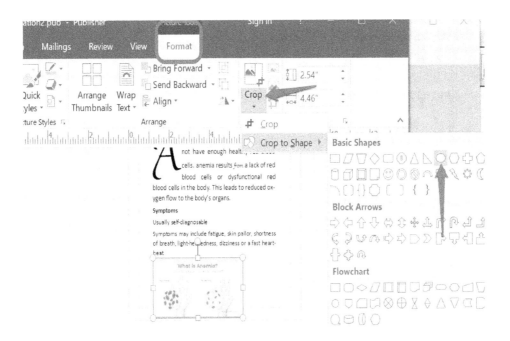

Then choose a shape from the slideout.

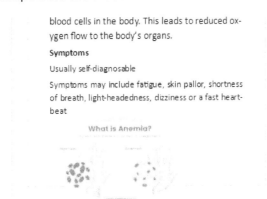

Adjusting Your Images

You can modify the contrast and brightness of your images or re-color them so that the image will fit into your color blueprint. To regulate or adjust an image follow the steps below.

1. Right-click on the image.
2. Select 'format picture'. From the popup menu.
3. From the dialog box, select the 'picture' tab.

You can now use the transparency slider to adjust the transparency of the image. Use the contrast and brightness sliders to adjust the contrast and brightness. To change the color of the image, use the re-color drop-down.

Click 'ok' when you are done.

Wrapping Text around images

When you import an image, the image will be wrapped naturally with text, which means that the text will position itself around the image rather than over it or beneath it.

Follow the steps below, to reform the text wrap

1. Click on the image.
2. Click 'wrap text' from the format tab.
3. Select 'tight' from the drop-down list to arrange the text exactly around the border of the image.
4. Click and drag the image into position if you wish to. You will observe that the text will align itself around the image.

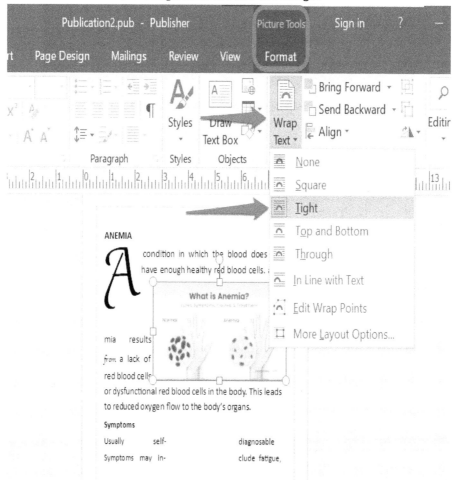

Wrapping points

Follow the steps below if you want to design the points at which the text wraps the image.

1. Click on the image
2. Click 'wrap text' from the format ribbon.
3. Then from the drop-down menu select 'edit wrap point'.

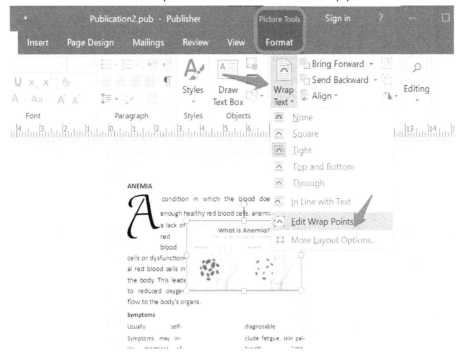

4. You will notice a dotted line appear displayed around the image. It is called the **wrap point.** Click and drag the dots to edit it.

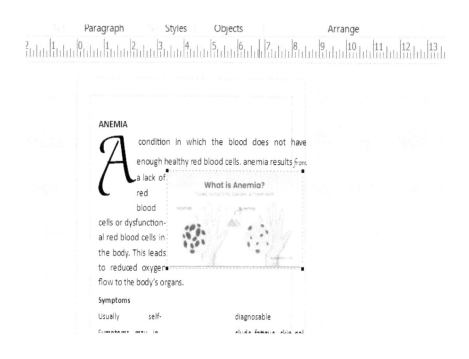

Adding Shapes To Your Publication

You can add diverse different shapes to your publication. You can also add lines, circles, rectangles, squares, and speech bubbles, you can also add diverse flow chart symbols.

Select the 'insert tab' to insert a shape.

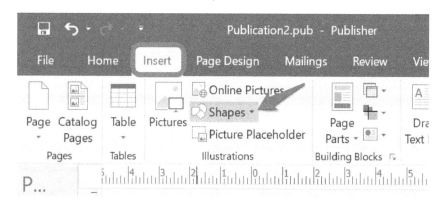

Choose the shape from the drop-down list.

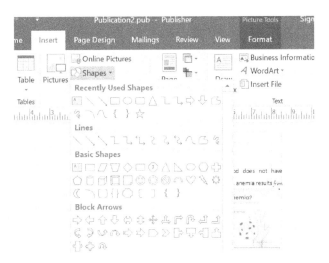

You will have to click and drag your mouse on your document to create your shape.

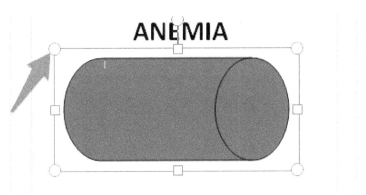

Altering Shapes

The color and the outline can be changed and also add shadows to your shapes.

Changing The Color

Follow the steps beneath to change this

1. Click on the shape

2. Choose the 'drawing tools' format tab.
3. Choose 'fill color', then pick a color from the drop-down list.

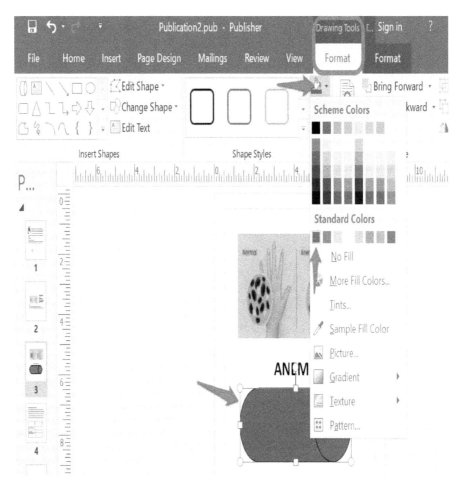

If you like to add a gradient, choose 'gradient' from the drop-down list. And if you also want to add a texture, pick 'texture'

Changing The Border

If you want to change this, click on your image, then pick the 'drawing tools' format tab. Pick 'shape outline', then select a color.

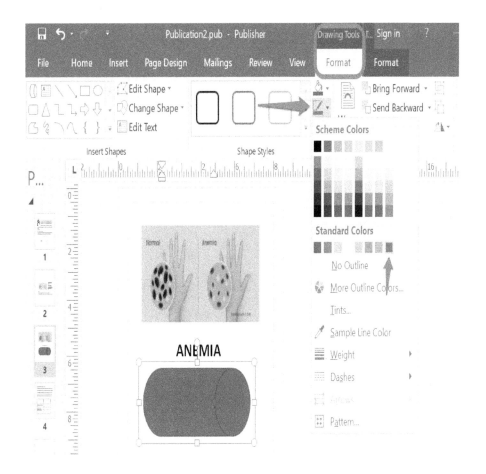

Choose 'weight' if you want to change the thickness of the border.

Adding a Shadow

Click on the image, then click on the 'drawing tools' format tab.

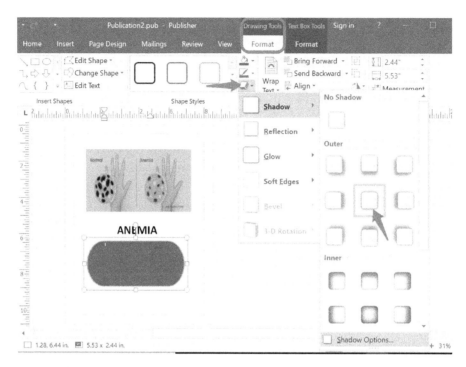

Choose 'shape effects', then pick an effect from the drop-down list. If you want to edit the effect, move down to 'option' at the base of the slideout menu.

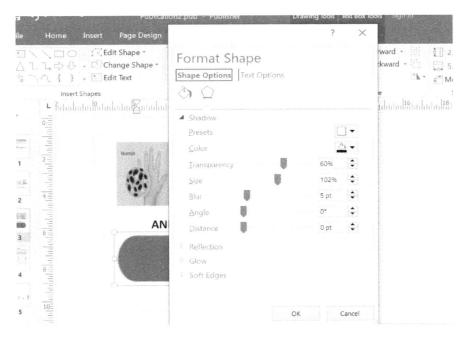

Adjust your effect by using the sliders.

Objects Alignment

You can naturally align objects on your page. Follow the steps below to do this.

1. Select the objects you want to align.
2. Hold down the control key on the keyboard while you click on the images you want to align.
3. Pick the 'picture tools' format tab
4. and click 'Arrange'
5. click align

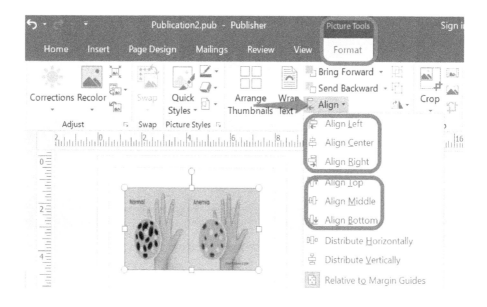

Pick an option from the drop-down list. Either Align Left, Align Centre, Align Right, Align Top, Align Middle, or Align Bottom.

When you pick Align Left it will align the left side of the objects with the left edge of the leftmost chosen object. You can also try all other aligns to see what the object would look like.

Objects Distribution

You can involuntarily distribute numerous objects equally across your page. To perform this, click all the objects you want to distribute. Press long the control key on the keyboard while you click on the images you want to distribute.

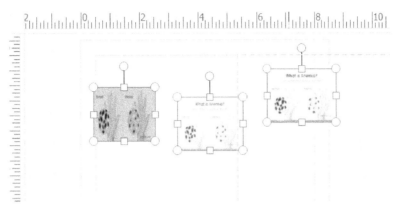

Pick the 'picture tools' format tab and choose 'arrange'. Select 'align'

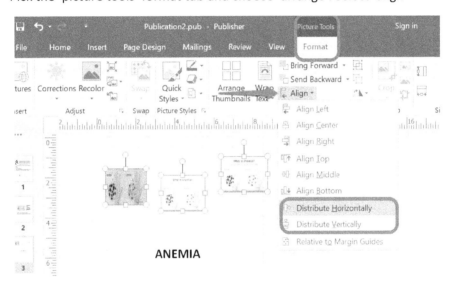

Choose either to distribute vertically or distribute horizontally from the drop-down list. Distributing horizontally will shift the selected objects an equal length apart horizontally all over your selection.

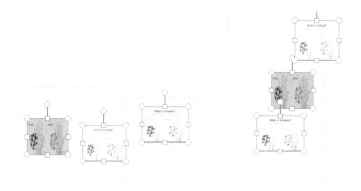

Distributing vertically will shift the selected objects an equal length apart vertically all over your selection.

Grouping Objects

You can cluster numerous objects into one object for them to stay together. This is very helpful if you have formed a graphic made up of numerous shapes and objects so you can resize and shift without having to change each shape. And if you want to do this, click all the objects you want to cluster. Press long the control key on the keyboard while you are clicking on the images.

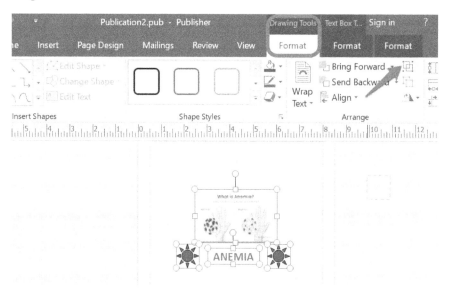

Choose the 'picture tools' or 'drawing tools' format tab then click 'group'.

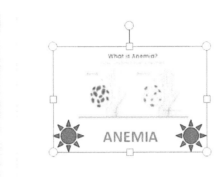

You can now easily move the graphic as a single object. If you want to ungroup, click on the object then select 'ungroup' from the 'drawing tools' or the 'picture tools'.

Positioning Object Layers

Publications are created using crystalline layers. Whenever you add an object, image, text box, or shape, it will have a new layer at the top. Check this for instance:

So we can now have a layer like this:

Page parts

The publisher has various pre-designed building blocks to assist you in designing your page. You can swiftly add sidebars or titles to your page and also preformatted quotes and stories. Follow the steps below to add a page part:

1. click the insert tab.
2. Click on page parts.
3. Select a template from the drop-down list.

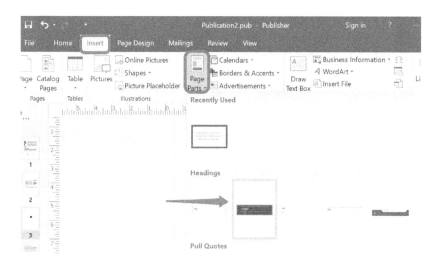

4. Click and drag the page part into bearings and resize it if needed.

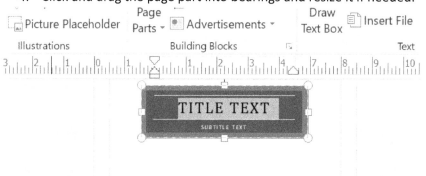

You can now type in your text in the placeholders.

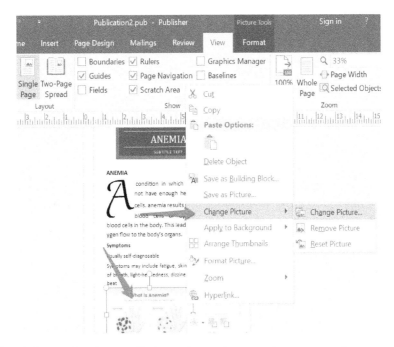

Right-click on the image if there is an image, then move downward to 'change picture' and choose 'change picture' from the slideout.

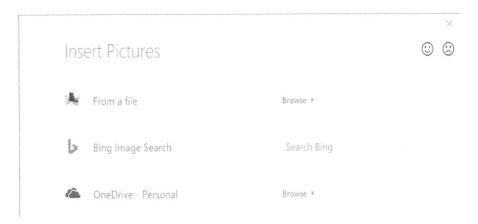

Choose where you would like to input your picture, then pick your picture.

If you would like to change the colors. Click on the page part, and select the 'drawing tools' format tab.

From this place you can make use of the shape fill to adjust the fill color, shape outline to adjust the border colors, and shape effects to include shadows or reflections to the page part.

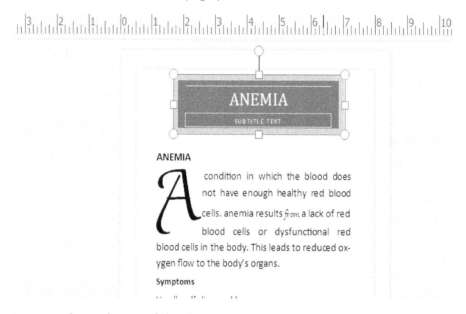

You can also make use of the shape-style programs on this ribbon tab.

Pick one and give it a trial.

Adding Borders and Accents

You can include borders on your page, text box, or image. You can also include accents which are tiny decorations that can be used to stress other objects. if you want to add an accent, click on the insert tab then select borders and accents.

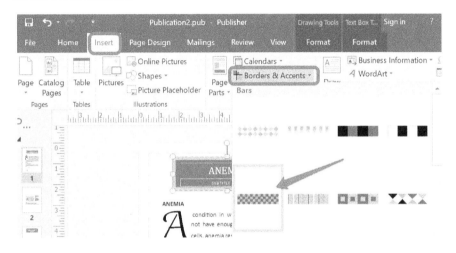

Recale and move the accent to where you want it to be.

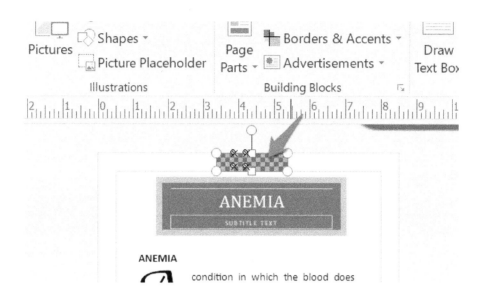

Inserting Calendars Into Your Publisher

If you want to include a calendar, click on the insert tab then click 'calendars' and pick a template from the drop-down list.

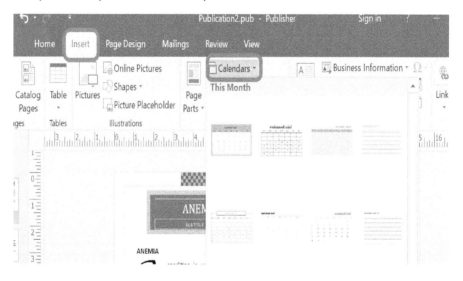

Rescale and shift your calendar into place.

May 2023

Sun	Mon	Tue	Wed	Thu	Fri	Sat
	1	2	3	4	5	6
7	8	9	10	11	12	13
14	15	16	17	18	19	20
21	22	23	24	25	26	27
28	29	30	31			

For instance, if you want to include a calendar with a precise month, select 'more calendar' from the calendar drop-down list.

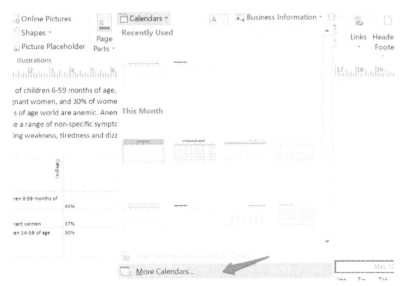

Pick a blueprint or format, then input the month and the year into the box on the right-hand side. Click on 'insert' when you are through.

Creating Of Advertisements

You can speedily create ads, free offers, attention grabbers, and coupons. For you to do this you have to follow the steps below

1. Click on the Insert tab.
2. Select 'advertisements' then pick a format from the drop-down list.
3. To able to see all the ads format click on 'more advertisements' at the base.

Resize and shift the ad into place on your page.

Type your details into the text boxes.

If you want to change any images, you have to right-click on the image, then choose 'change image' from the slideout, then Choose where you want to input your picture, and then pick your picture.

Adding WordArt

WardArt is applicable for making headings and eye-catching text. To include WordArt, click on the 'insert' tab then select 'WordArt'. pick a style from the drop-down list.

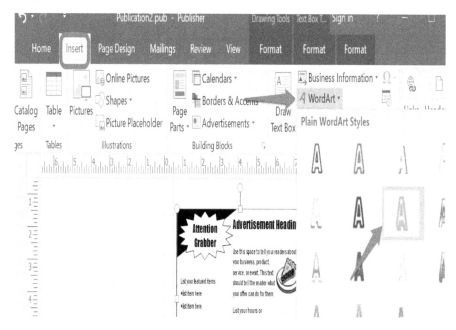

Choose your font and size then input your WordArt text.

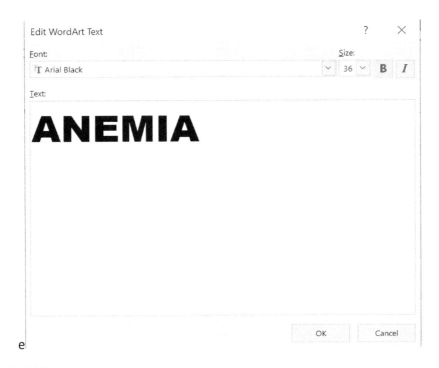

Edit WordArt Text	? ✕

Font: Size:

T Arial Black ∨   36 ∨   **B** *I*

Text:

ANEMIA

OK   Cancel

e

Click 'ok'

You can change the style of the text using the sets up from the WordArt tools format tab,

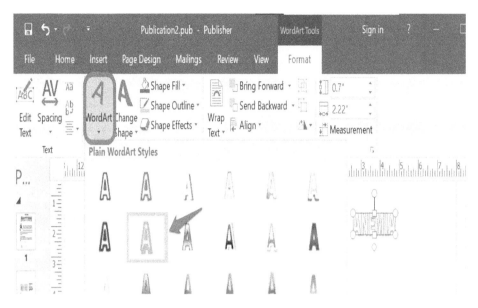

Include a reflection or shadow effect using 'shape effects'.

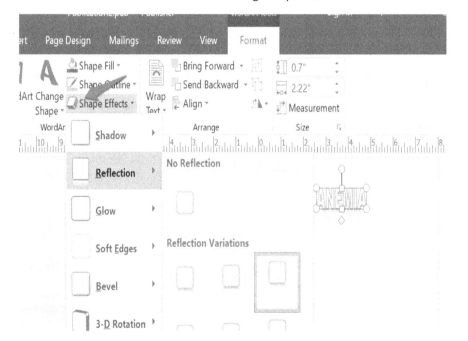

By using the 'fill color' you can modify the color.

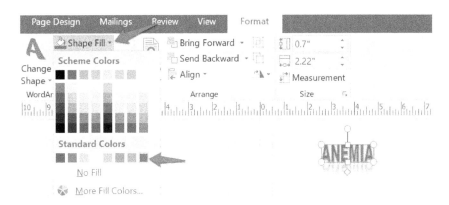

Adjust the border of the text using 'shape outline'.

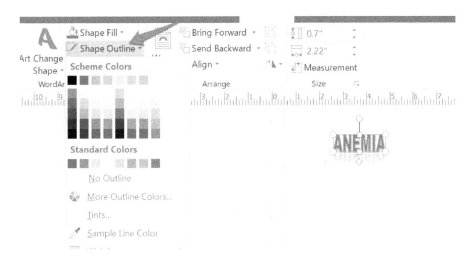

If you want to change the shape of the text. Click 'change shape'. Choose a shape from the drop-down list.

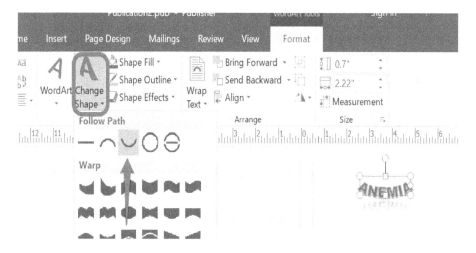

To reform the shape, click and drag the small yellow handle on the WordArt.

Use the resize handles to rescale your WordArt, and use the rotate handle to turn your WordArt.

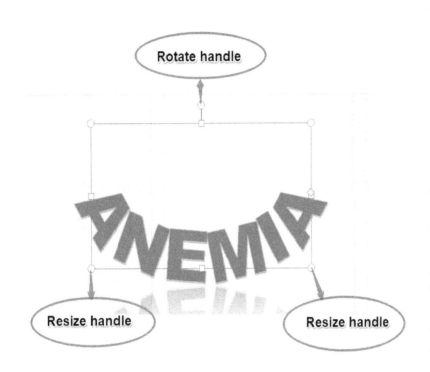

Chapter Five

Creating Mail Merge

In this segment, we shall be taking a look at creating a mail merge to create addressed envelopes and invites using a publisher.

Creating A Mail Marge Envelopes

If you have many recipients, creating an envelope for each of them can be time compelling. This is the reason why mail merge is helpful. To do this, you will have to open an envelope pattern or create one. Click 'new' on the start-up screen, click on 'built-in' then Go down and choose 'envelope'.

Go down to 'blank sizes' and choose the size of the envelope you will be using. Select 'create'.

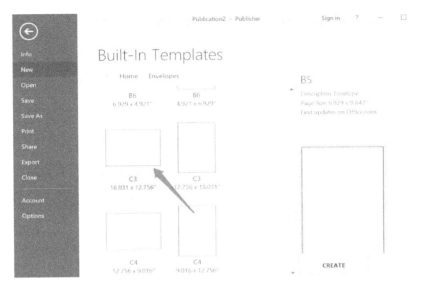

The next thing you will need now is a data source and it is mainly a list of names and addresses. The best place to store names and addresses is in an Excel spreadsheet. There is one of my clients list that I keep in an Excel spreadsheet, therefore in this example, I will make use of it. You can also follow the same method if you use your Outlook contacts.

To choose a data source, move to your mailings tab and click 'select recipients'.

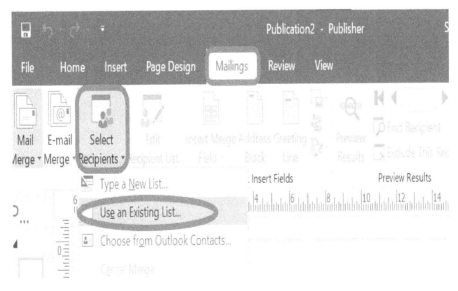

From the drop-down list, click 'use an existing list…'.

Find your data source from the dialog box that comes into sight, I will choose my Excel spreadsheet. Mail Merge Data1

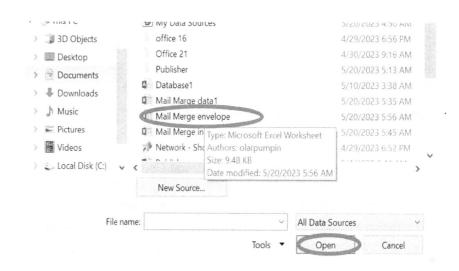

Click 'open'

Then click 'ok' on the next two dialog boxes that appear.

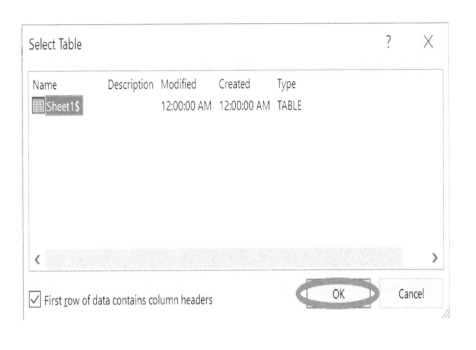

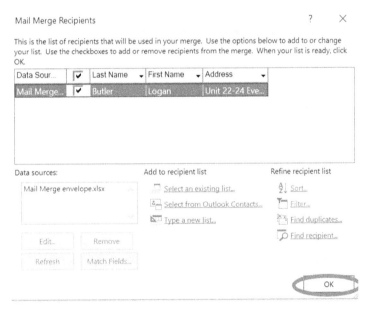

To create your envelopes, choose 'address block' from the mailings tab, to add the addresses from your contacts data source.

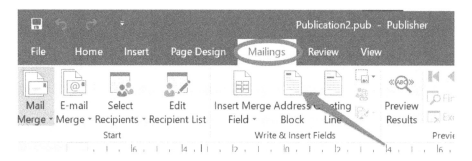

Rescale your address block...

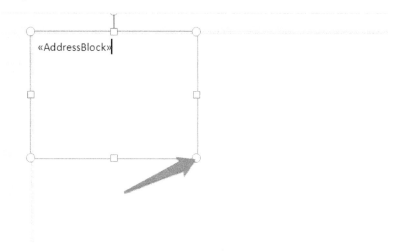

To sample your envelopes, from the Mailings tab select 'preview results'. By using the next/previous record icons, you can turn over through the envelopes.

To carry out your action to the end, from the Mailings tab click 'finish and merge'. From the drop-down list, select 'print documents' to send a large of it to the printer, make sure that you have already loaded your envelopes into your printer's paper tray.

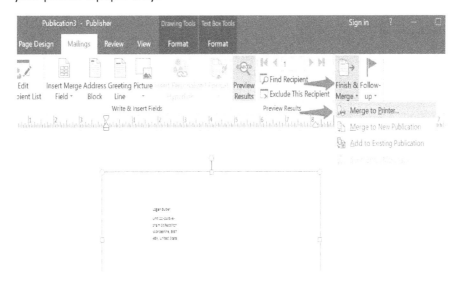

You can also pick 'edit individual documents' and Word will create a document with all your envelopes set to print. This is helpful if you only want to print certain addresses or make some adjustments.

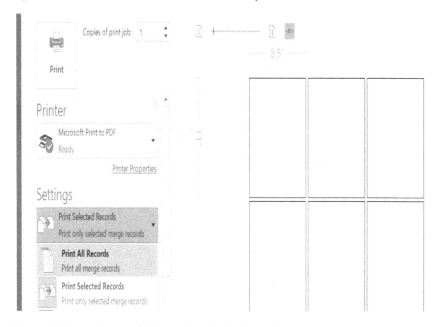

Choose 'print all records' from the dialog box that appears.

Creating Mail Merge Invitation

Now that our envelopes have been printed, we need to produce our party invitation. To do this, open a pattern. Click 'new' on the publisher's start screen, and type in the publication pattern you want in the search area. So I will be putting a birthday party in the search area.

Then double-click on the pattern you want.

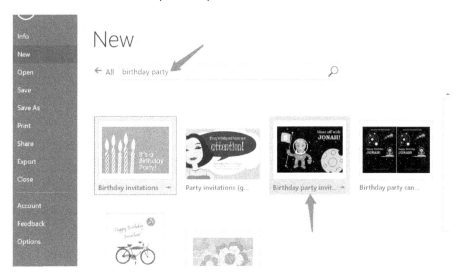

The next thing is to add your data source. To attach your data source, click on your mailings tab and choose 'select recipients'. Then select 'use an existing list' from the drop-down menu.

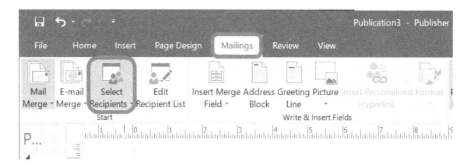

Then choose your data file.

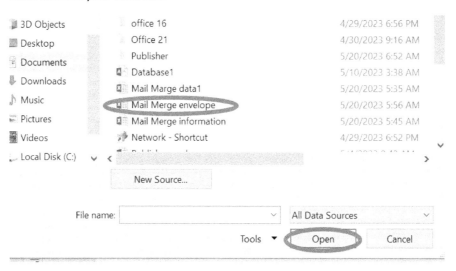

Click open on the dialog box. We can begin to add names now. Select 'insert merge field', from the mailings tab. Then from the drop-down select 'first_name', click 'insert merge field', and choose 'last_name'.

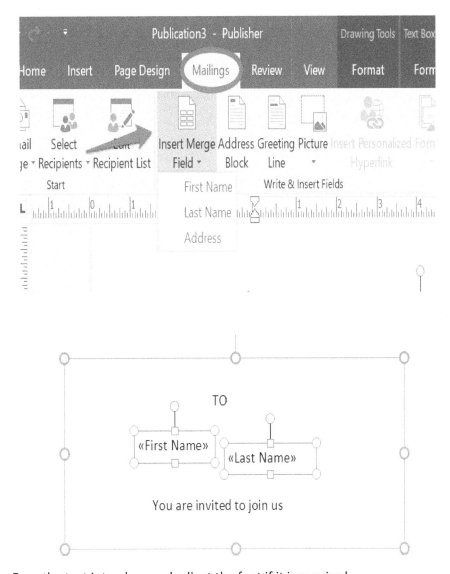

Drag the text into place and adjust the font if it is required.

Once you have included all the fields, from the mailings tab select 'preview results'. You will have something like this (an individualized invitation for each name):

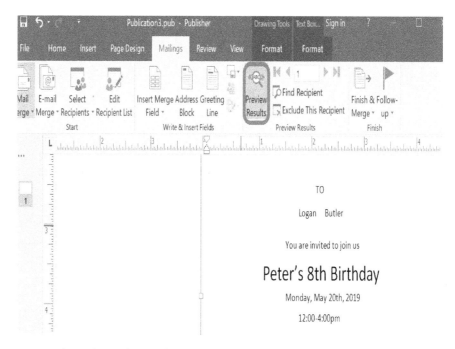

To complete, from the mailings tab, click 'finish & merge'

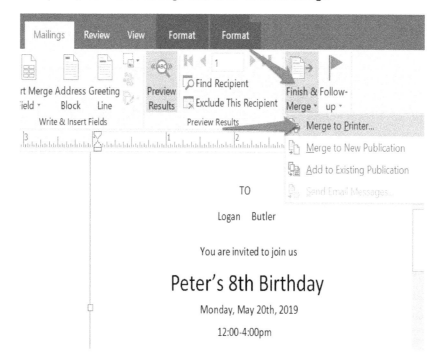

select 'print document' to send all the letters to the printer.

Using Pre-designed Templates

In this excerpt, we shall be looking at various diverse pre-designed templates that come with the publisher, as well as building a template from scratch.

Finding a Pre-designed Template

When you turn on the publisher, you will notice a screen comprising thumbnails of diverse templates that are obtainable. To locate the template, click 'new' on the left-hand side.

The best method to locate templates is to search for them.

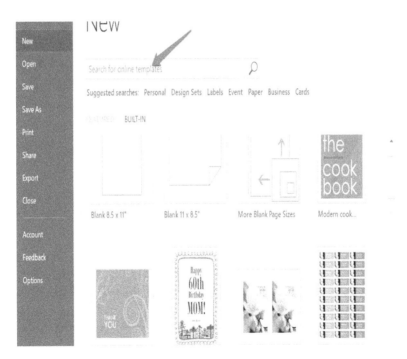

Why not try creating a greeting card for somebody that you know so well?

Open publisher, select 'new' on the left-hand side, then type... **Birthday card** into the search area

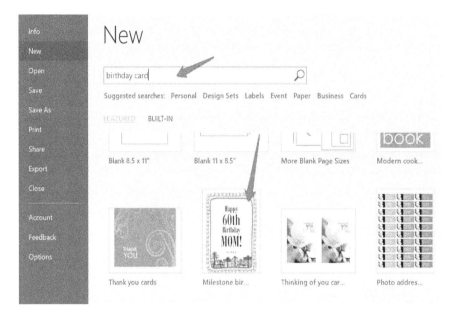

Choose a template to use from the search outcome. How about a lovely Birthday card?

Double-click on the template thumbnail.

The text or photo can be changed.

You just have to click on the text and enter your own.

Making Your Template

If you have built your style, e.g. fonts, heading sizes, and layouts, you can store this as a template, so you can build new documents in the same style.

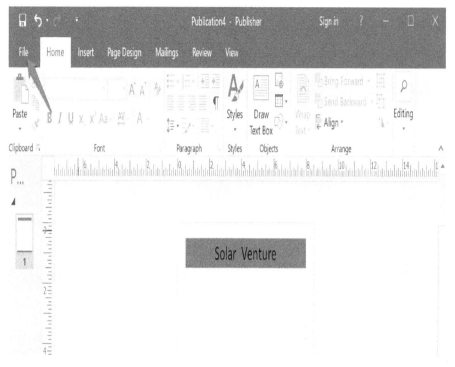

To keep your publication as a template, select 'file' on the top left. Select 'save as' from the backstage menu. Choose your 'Onedrive' folder. From the popup 'save as' dialog box, scroll down to 'save as type'. Turn this to 'publisher template', then click 'save'. To open a new file using the pattern, from the publisher start screen, click 'new'. Go down and choose 'personal'. Double-click your pattern. You are now free to type in your text. If you want to save it as a new publication, click 'file' on the top left of the screen. Select 'save as'. Choose a folder to save your document in, and give the file a significant.

Chapter Six

Managing Publication

In this excerpt, we will look at the following: saving your work, printing, page setup, and page masters.

To save your work, click on the **File** at the top left-hand side of the screen.

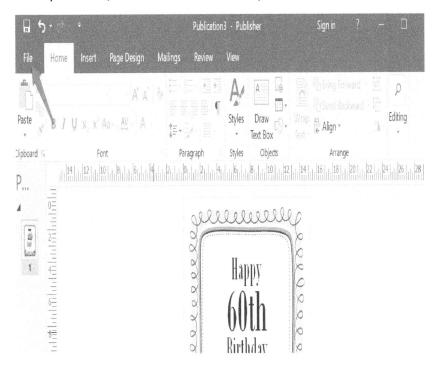

Pick 'save as' on the left-hand side. You will need to let the publisher know where to save the document, in the save as screen. You need to double-click on **This PC**, then select where you want to keep your publication from the dialog box (e.g. in 'document').

Then you need to give your file a name, on this occasion 'Birthday card'. Select 'save'

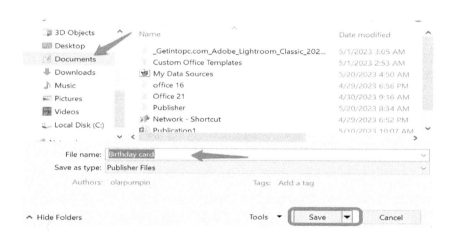

Saving your publication as a Different Format

Occasionally you will want to keep a document in a different format. This can be helpful if you are transmitting a document to someone who might not have Microsoft Office installed or who might not be using Windows.

Publisher permits you to keep your document in diverse formats. A familiar illustration is saving files as PDFs, which is a mobile format that can be read on any type of computer, phone, or tablet without having Microsoft Publisher installed.

With your document open, select the **file** on the top left of the screen. Choose 'save as' from the list on the left-hand side.

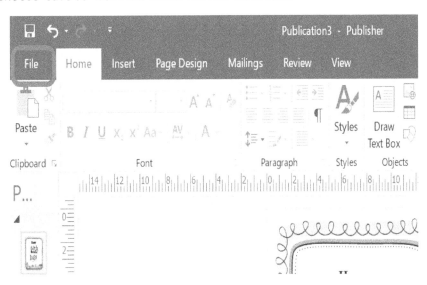

Double-click 'This PC', and choose the folder you will like to save your work into. Eg 'documents'.

Give your file a nice name, in this event 'Birthday card'.

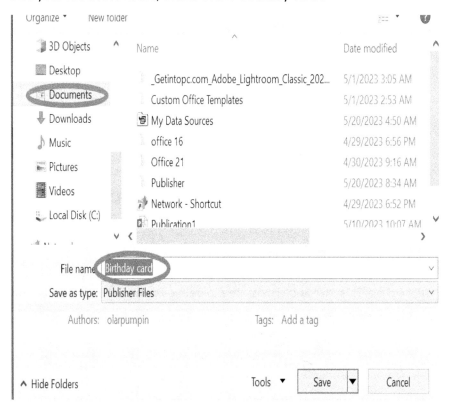

To change the format, click on the down arrow in the field below, then from the list select PDF.

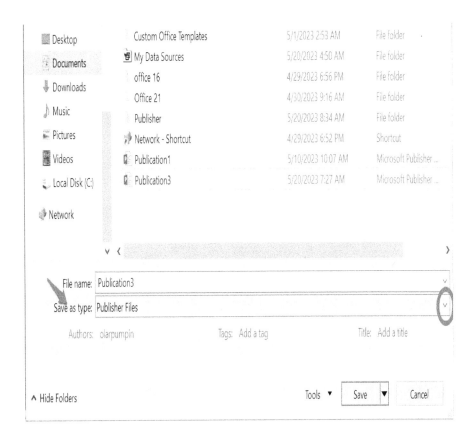

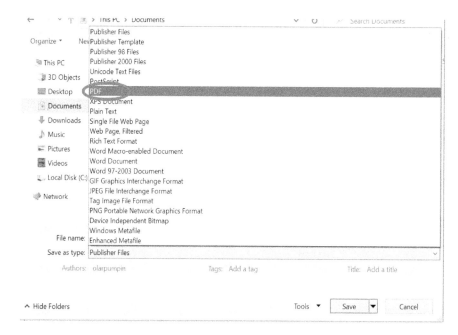

Then click 'Save'.

Opening Saved Documents

In case you have already opened Publisher you can open formerly or previously saved documents, just click on the 'file tab' on your screen at the top left side.

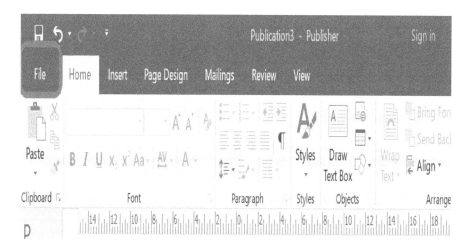

Click 'open' from the green bar.

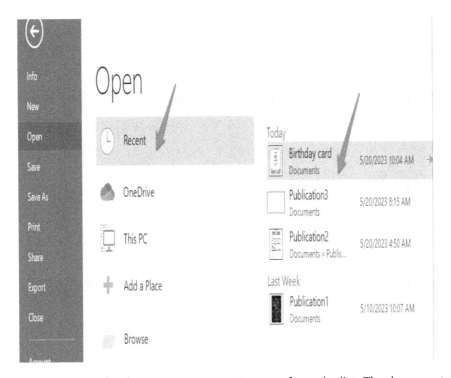

You can choose the document you want to open from the list. The document from the former project was stored as 'Birthday card.pub', so I will open this particular one.

For comfort, Microsoft Publisher lists all your newly opened documents. Your newest files will be listed first. Double-click the file name to open it.

For instance, if your document is kept on your PC, double-click on the PC icon to browse the files. Choose your file.

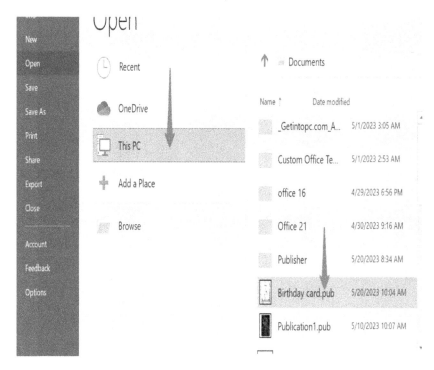

Click 'open'.

Using Page Setup

Page setup permits you to modify the paper size, margins, orientation (portrait/landscape), and general layout.

To modify your page setup, move to your 'page design' tab and select the expand icon on the underside right of the page setup area.

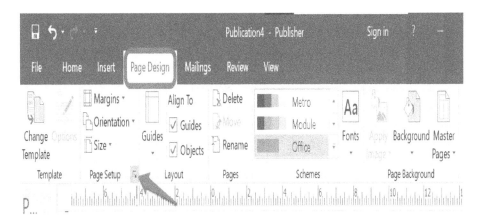

From the dialog box that comes up, you can adjust the layout type meaning you can make a booklet layout, full page, envelope, etc.

You can change the margins as shown beneath using the 'margin guide'.

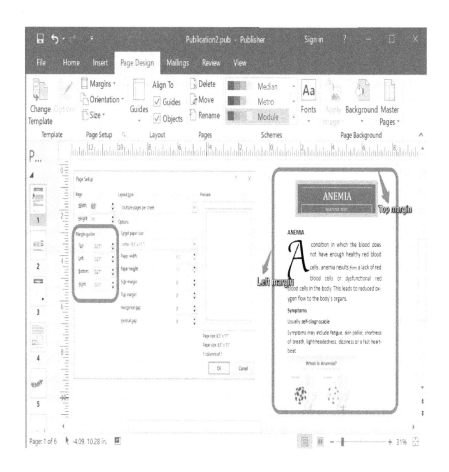

You can also change the page size.

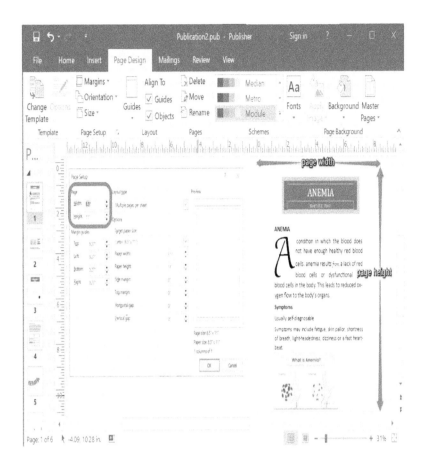

Creating Booklets

To make a booklet layout, first, open a blank publication. From the page design tab, select the icon on the underside at the right of the 'page setup' area.

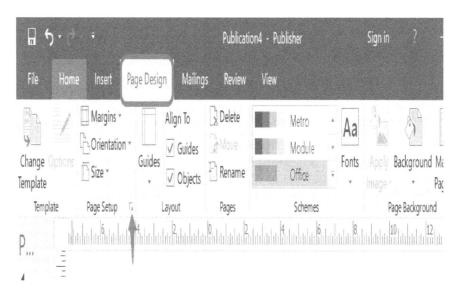

Select 'booklet' in the 'page setup' dialog box, under 'layout type'.

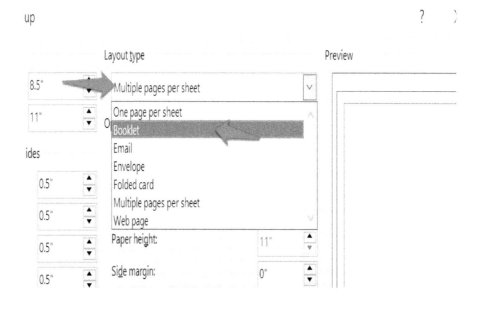

When you click 'ok' the Publisher will make a booklet layout for you. You will notice your pages in the navigation pane on the left-hand side of the screen. Here, you have your front page, the inside spread, and the back page.

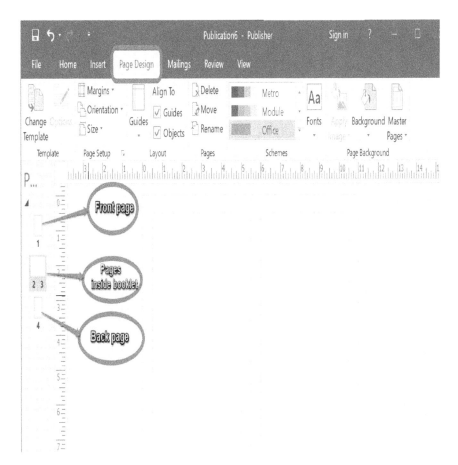

Now you can start to create your booklet. This is an adequate way to start. If you transform a Publisher document to booklet form you may encounter problems with layout if Publisher needs to resize pages.

Using Page Masters

Page Masters permits you to repeat layout elements and design on multiple pages in a publication. This creates a more constant appearance throughout your work and permits you to update the design in a single place, rather than changing them on each page.

Editing Master Pages

For illustration, if you are making a booklet, you can include page numbers or page headers on each page.

Add a header such as a title

Include a footer. Click on the footer of the page.

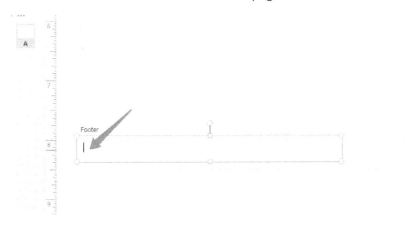

Include a page number, and click on the 'insert page number'.

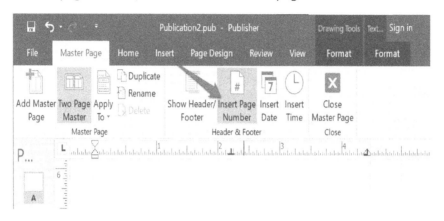

Creating Master Pages

To make a new master, click on the 'page design' tab, then select 'add master page'.

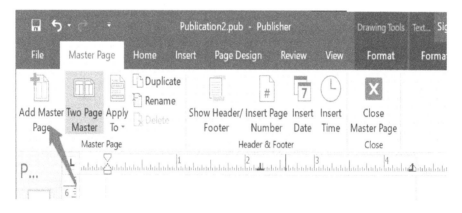

You can give a descriptive name to the master in the 'description' area. Click 'ok'.

If you want the master to be a double-page spread, one you'd find in the center of the booklet, click 'two-page master'. If you just want a separate page, un-tick this option.

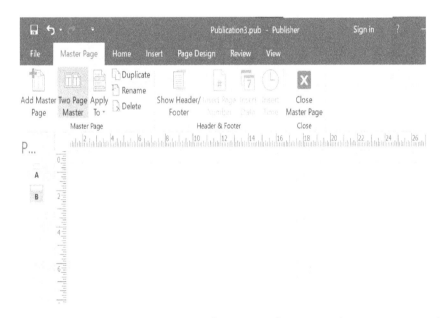

Now create your master. You can input text boxes or pictures as normal using the 'insert' tab.

Applying Master

Right-click on the page or spread in the navigation pane on the left-hand side if you want to apply a master to a page. Move down to 'master pages' and choose a master from the slideout list. If you want to use a master to numerous pages or a spectrum of pages, right-click on the page in the page navigation pane on the left. Scroll down to 'master pages', and pick 'apply master pages' from the slideout list. Pick the master you want to use from the dialog box. Choose the pages you would like to apply the master too, eg 'all pages'. Click 'ok'.

Inserting Guides

Layout guides enable you to distance out your publication, and text boxes, and align pictures, and tables. Layout guides come up on your page as a line or grid. There are certain guides you can use to set up your publication. To authorize them, click your 'page design' tab and select 'guides'.

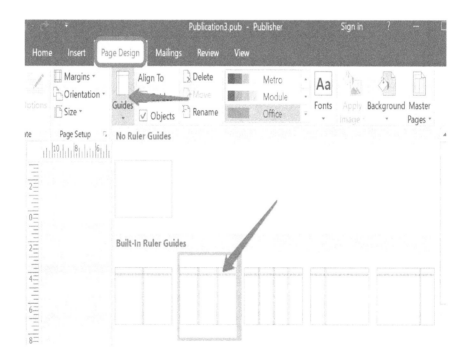

From the drop-down list, you can choose the setup you want. For instance, if you are developing a newsletter choose a double or three-column setup. Arrange your headings, text boxes, and pictures to the grid lines.

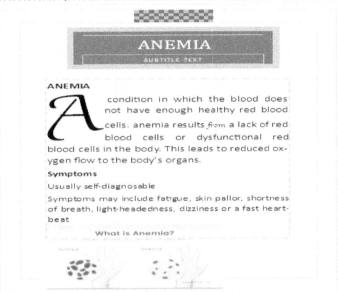

To move a setup line, click and drag it to a new place.

To include a setup line, click on the vertical ruler and drag the green setup line into place on the page.

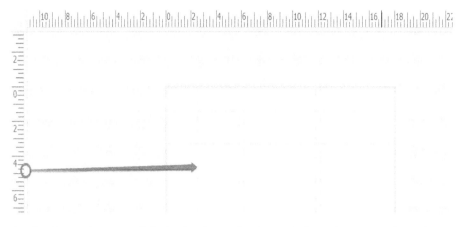

For horizontal setup, click the horizontal ruler and drag the green down into place on the page.

To delete a setup line, right-click on the line and select 'delete guide'

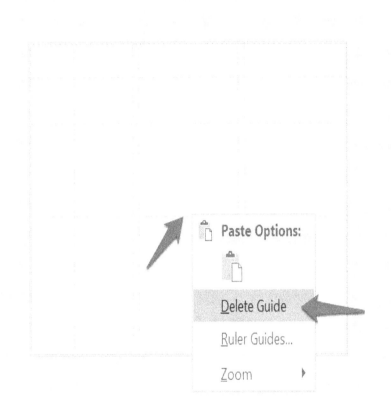

Chapter Seven

Publishing your Work

Will you be Publishing electronically? Printing? In this area, we will be taking a look at exporting, printing, and sharing your publication.

Printing Your Documents

Click 'file' on the top left of your screen.

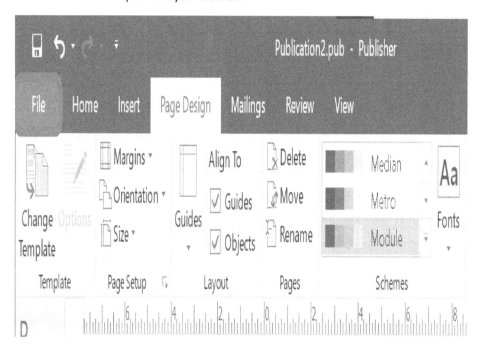

Choose 'print' from the green bar on the left-hand side of the screen.

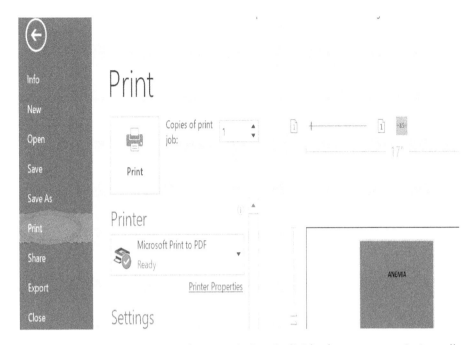

You can choose options such as: printing individual pages or printing all pages and the number of copies. You can print numerous pages on a single sheet print the page on a single sheet of paper or scale it up to numerous sheets. You can also print the pages into a booklet. To adjust the setting click the 'one page per sheet' drop-down list.

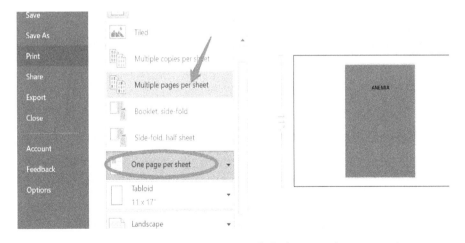

After you have selected all your options, click the print button at the top.

Printing as Booklet

Open your publication. Click on the 'file' on the top left of the screen to print as a booklet.

Click 'print' from the green bar on the left-hand side of the screen.

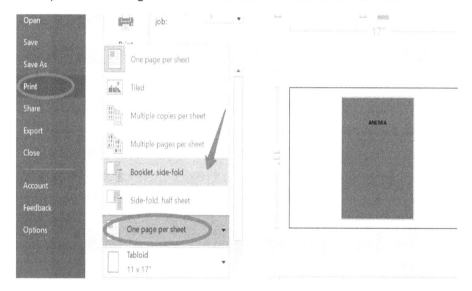

From the 'settings' area, scroll down to 'one page per sheet'. From the drop-down list, choose 'booklet side fold'.

Most current printers support double printing (i.e. printing on both sides of the paper). With several desktop printers, choosing a duplex means that the printer prints all the copies of the first side of a page, then stops and asks you to turn around the sheets that it just printed and return them to the printer. Then all the copies of the second side would be printed.

To print on both sides, you will have to click on the drop-down box that says 'print one-sided'

Click 'print' at the top of the screen.

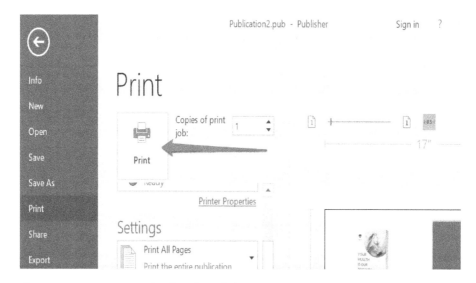

If you want to print on both sides of the page, immediately after the printer has printed the first page, turn the whole stack of the printed sheets over and return them to the paper tray.

Exporting Your Work as a PDF

Click on the file at the top left of your screen.

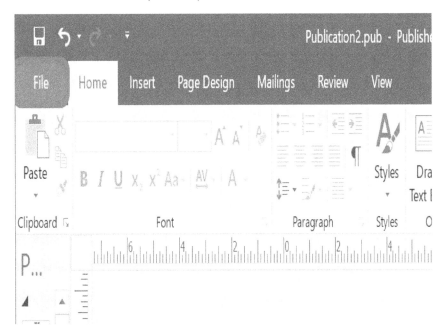

Choose 'export' from the left-hand side. Select 'Create PDF/XPS Document', then click on the 'Create PDF/XPS' button.

Choose where you want to save the PDF file, give it a relevant name, then click on 'publish'.

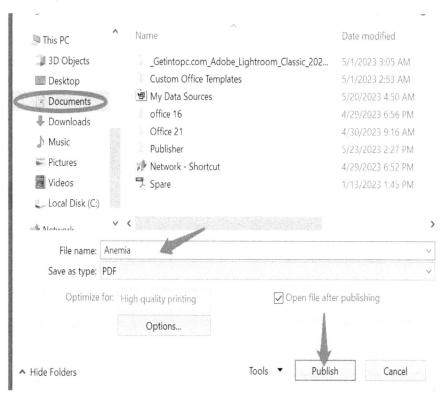

Share a File

Click the file on the left-hand side of the screen.

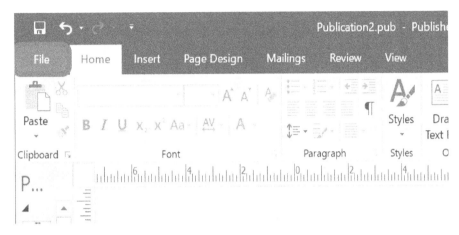

Choose 'share' from the list on the left-hand side.

Select how you want to connect the file to your email. You can send the latest page as an email, you can send your publication as a publisher file (.pub), or you can transmit the file as a PDF. If you are transmitting the file to someone who does not have a publisher installed, you need to send the file as a PDF. For instance, I would like to send it as PDF. So I will have to click 'send as PDF'. Immediately after the email opens up, you will notice the file connected to the email. Add the email address of the receiver and include a subject and a message.

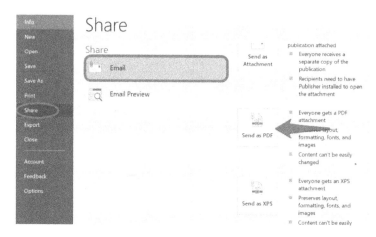

Click 'send' when you are through.

BOOK TWO: MICROSOFT ACCESS

CHAPTER ONE

Getting Started with Access

Access can be irreplaceable for storing and organizing customer lists, addresses, inventories, payment histories, volunteer lists, and donor lists. This chapter presents databases and the concepts behind databases. It displays how to create a database and database tables for storing information.

The other aspect of this chapter shows you how to design databases. You need to be aware of database design before you can start dealing with databases. You can just rush in as you always do with the other Office programs.

Access provides a practical database known as Northwind that you can test with as you get to navigate around databases. To unlock this database, kindly follow the steps below.

➤ Click the File tab.

➢ Choose New.

➢ Then in the New window, enter **Northwind** in the Search box.

➢ Click the Start Searching button.

Understanding Database

The address book on your computer is a database, so likewise the telephone directory in the desk drawer. A recipe book is also a database, anywhere information is stored systematically can be considered a database. What makes a difference between a computerized database and a conventional database is that storing, manipulating, and finding data is easier in a computerized database.

You need to know how data is stored in a database and how it is extracted, to use database terminology. You must know about objects, Access's bland word for database tables, queries, forms, and all things that make a database a database. These pages provide a crash course in databases. They clarify the different objects—tables, queries, forms, and reports—that make up a database.

Database tables for storing information

Information in databases is stored in database tables like the one in the image below. You include one field for each category of information you want to keep on hand. Fields are the equivalent of columns in a table.

The first duty you need to carry out when you create a database is to name the fields and inform Access what kind of information you suggest to store in each field. The database table below is for storing employee information. It has seven fields: ID, First Name, Last Name, E-mail Address, Business Phone, Company, and Job Title.

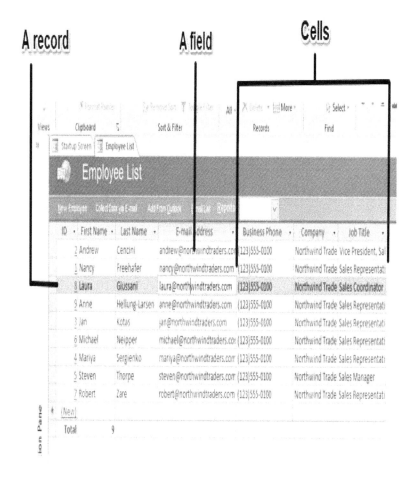

Forms for entering data

You can start entering the records after you create the fields in the database table. A record explains all the data concerning one person or thing. You can enter records directly into a database table, the easiest way to input a record is with a **form.** see the image below:

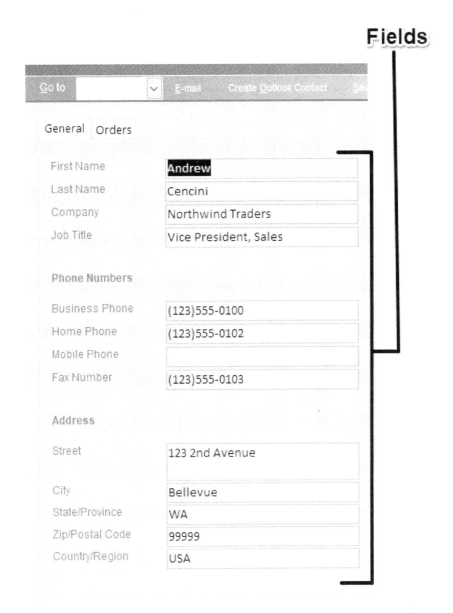

Queries for accomplishing the data out

A query is a question you ask of a database; in an address database, you can use a query to discover all the people in a particular ZIP code or state. If information about contributions is kept in the database, you can find out who contributed more than $400 last month. After you create a query, you can save it and run it again.

Reports for offering and inspecting data

Reports can be made from database tables or the results of queries. They are usually read by managers and others who do not get their hands muddy in the database. They are meant to be printed and distributed so that the information can be inspected and examined. Access provides numerous attractive reports.

Macros and modules

Macros and modules are not discussed in this book, but they are also database objects. A macro is a series of commands. You can store macros for running queries and carrying out other Access tasks. A module is a group of Visual Basic procedures and declarations for carrying out tasks in Access.

Generating a Database File

Generating a database is a lot of work, Access provides two ways to create a new database file. You can get the help of a template or do it from scratch. With a template, some of them are done for you. The template comes with manufactured forms, queries, and reports. However, templates are for those who already know their way around databases. You have to know how to change a preexisting database if you want to make use of a template.

Generating a blank database file

Follow the steps below to generate a blank database file:

1. Click the file tab or Access opening screen, then select New.

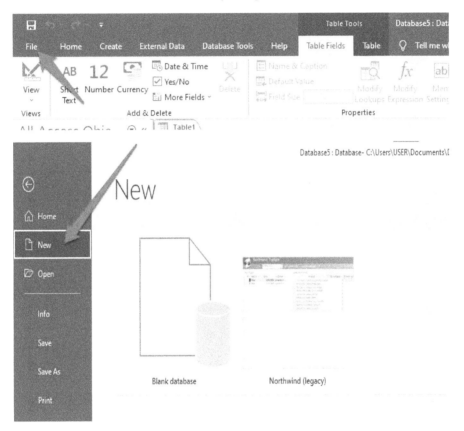

2. Click the Blank Database icon.

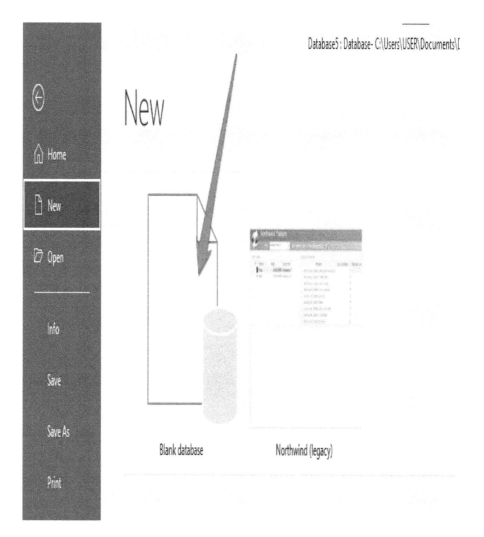

Database5 : Database- C:\Users\USER\Documents\[

Blank database   Northwind (legacy)

3. Click the Browse button

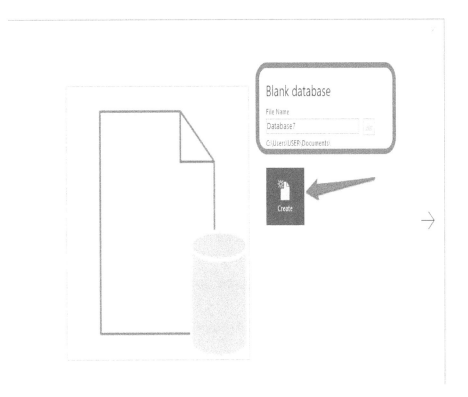

4. Choose the folder where you want to store the database file, then input a name in the File Name text box, and click OK.

5. Click the Create button.

Obtaining the assistance of a template

To obtain the help of a template, kindly follow these steps to a database from a template:

1. Select New on the File tab, or Access opening screen.

2. Choose a template or use the search box to obtain a template online from Microsoft.

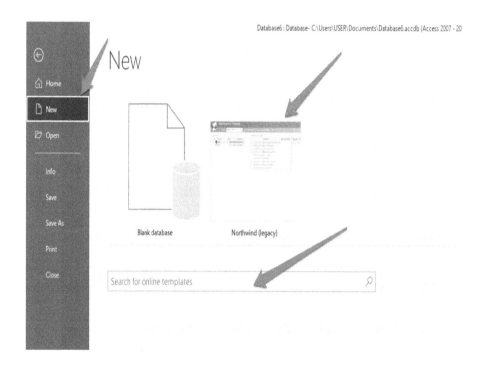

3. Click the Browse button.

4. Choose the folder where you want to store the database file, insert a name in the File Name text box, and then click OK.

5. Click the Create button.

Moving Around the Navigation Pane

The first thing that appears when you unlock most database files is called the Navigation pane see the image below:

This is the starting point for carrying out all your work in Access. From here you can choose an object. Tables, queries, and other objects you create are added to the Navigation pane when you create them. Below are the instructions for doing this, that, and other things in the Navigation pane:

➤ **Selecting an object type:** choose a group (Tables, Queries, Forms, Reports, and so on) from the Object Type drop-down list above the Navigation pane, or choose All Access Objects to view all the groups.

➤ **Generating a new object:** move to the Create tab and select what type of object you want to create. When generating new forms and reports, click a table or query in the Navigation pane to base the new form or report on a table or query.

➤ **Unlocking an object:** To unlock a database table, form, report, or query, do one of the following: choose it and press Enter; Double-click it; or right-click it and select Open on the shortcut menu.

➤ **Unlocking an object in the Design view:** the job of formulating database tables, forms, and queries is done in the Design view. In case an object requires reformulating, right-click it and select Design View on the shortcut menu or click the Design View beneath the screen.

➤ **Unlocking and closing the Navigation pane:** Click the Shutter Bar Open/Close button above the screen of the Navigation pane (or press F11) when you want to shrink it and get it out of the way. You can also resize this pane by clicking the far-right edge and dragging it right or left.

➤ **Finding objects:** Use the Search bar to look for objects, The Search bar can be located at the top of the Navigation pane.

Designing a database

To be a database designer is not nearly as fashionable as being a fashion designer, but there are rewards for it. It can be very helpful to you and others if you design your database correctly and carefully. You can enter information precisely. These pages describe all you need to take into consideration when designing a database.

Determining what information you want

The essential question to ask yourself is about the kind of information you want to obtain from the database. Sales information? Customer names and addresses? You can also interview your colleagues to find out what information could be useful to them.

Think about it seriously. Your focus is to set up the database so that every piece of information your organization needs can be recorded. The best way to find out what kind of information matters to an organization is to scrutinize the forms that the organization uses to implore or record information.

Plans for database tables and field names

Players
Players
Player Number
First Name
Last Name
Street address
City
State
Zip
Telephone
Email
Team Name
Fee paid
Birthday
Sex
School

Teams
Teams
Team Name
Division Number
Sponsor
Team Colors
Practice field
Practice Day
Practice Time

Division
Division
Division Number
Division Name

Coaches
Coaches
Coach Number
Team Name
First Name
Last Name
Street address
City
State
Zip
Telephone
Email
School

Separating information into diverse database tables

After you have gotten the information you need, you have to think about how to separate the information into database tables. To see how it works, consider the simple database in the table above.

The aim of this little database and its four tables is to store information about the players, coaches, and teams in a football league. The Team Name field appears in three tables. It serves as the link among the tables and allows more than one to be queried.

By querying individual tables in this database, I can gather team rosters, make a list of coaches and their contact information, list teams by division, place together a mailing list of all players, find out which players have paid their fees, and list players by age group, among other things. This database comprises four tables:

> **Players:** Comprises fields for tracking players' names, addresses, birthdays, which teams they are on, and if they paid their fees.

> **Coaches:** Comprises fields for tracking coaches' names, addresses, and the names of the teams they coach.

> **Teams:** Comprises fields for tracking team names and which division each team is in.

> **Divisions:** Comprises fields for tracking division numbers and names.

Determining how many database tables you need and how to separate data across diverse tables is the hardest aspect of designing a database. Below are the basic rules for separating data into diverse tables:

➢ **Avoid duplicate information:** Do not keep duplicate information in the same database table or duplicate information across diverse tables. By keeping the information in one place. You need to enter it once, and if you have to update it, you can do so in one database table, not numerous.

➢ **Restrict a table to one subject only:** Each database table should grasp information about one subject only—products, customers, and so on. This way you can preserve data in one table independently from data in another table.

Choosing fields for database tables

Fields are categories of information. Each database table needs at least one field. When you are planning which fields to include in a database table, follow the steps below:

➢ Break down the information into small elements. For instance, instead of a Name field, create a First Name field and a Last Name field.

➢ Give descriptive names to fields so that you know what they are later. A more descriptive name, such as Serial Number, is clearer than SN.

➢ Thing ahead and include a field for each bite of information your organization needs. Including a field in a database table late in the game is an inconvenience. You have to go back to each record, look up the information, and enter it.

➢ Do not put information that can be derived from a calculation. Calculations can be performed as part of a query or be made aspect of a table; this will be discussed in chapter four of this mini-book.

Deciding on a primary key field for each database table

Each database table must have a primary key field. This field, also known as the primary key, is the field in the database table where unique, one-of-a-kind data is kept. Data imputed in this field—a part number, and an employee ID number, must not be the same in each record. If you attempt to enter the same data in the primary key field of two different records, a dialog box warns you not to do that.

Primary key fields help Access recognize records and not collect the same information more than once in a query. Primary key fields prevent you from entering duplicate records. They also make queries more effective.

Invoice numbers and serial numbers make good primary key fields. Social security numbers also make excellent primary key fields.

Mapping the relationships between tables

You have to map how the tables relate to one another in case your database includes more than one table. Usually, relationships are formed between the primary key field in one table and the corresponding field in another, named the *foreign key.* See the tables below:

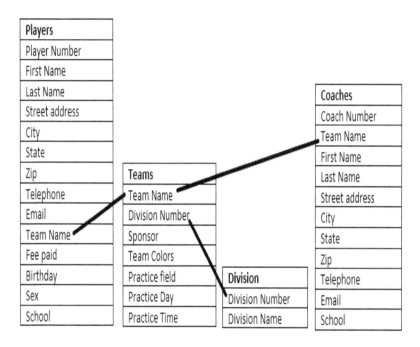

CHAPTER TWO

Constructing Your Database Tables

The building blocks of a database are the database tables. They grasp the raw data. You will have query access and generate reports from several different tables due to the relationships among the tables.

This chapter discusses how to create database tables, fields for the tables, and so on, in this chapter, you will discover several tricks and tips for making sure that data is entered correctly in your database.

Generating a database table

The first and most essential aspect of setting up a database is creating the tables and entering the data. Raw data is stored in database tables. Chapter one of this book discusses what database tables are and how to design an impressive one. Access provides three ways to create a database table:

- ➢ **Generate the database table from scratch:** Enter and format the fields one at a time by yourself.

- ➢ **Import the database table from another database:** This method can be a huge timesaver if you can reprocess data that has already been entered in a database table in another Access database.

- ➢ **Obtain the help of a template:** Obtain predesign fields assembled in a table. You can do this if you know Access well and you can change database tables and table fields.

Generating a database table from scratch

Here you create the tables and then enter the fields one after the other. After creating or opening a database file, kindly follow the instructions below to create a database table from scratch:

1. **Visit the Create tab.**

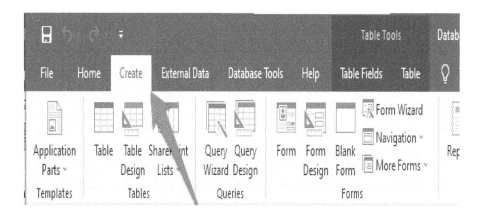

2. **Click the Table Design button.**

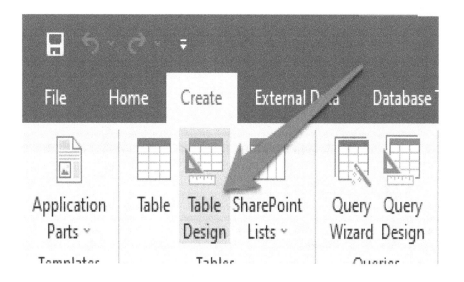

The Design window comes into sight. From here, you enter fields for your database table. See the image below.

3. **Click the Save button on the Quick Access toolbar.**

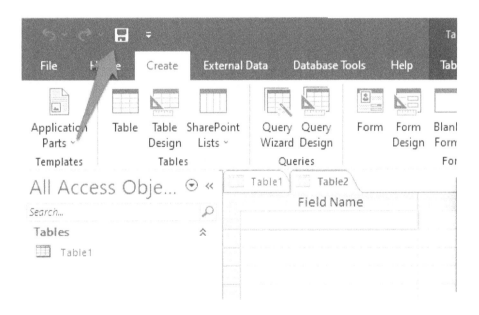

The Save As dialog box appears.

4. **Enter a descriptive name for your table and click ok.** When you go
   back to the Navigation pane you will see the name of the table you
   created. In case you do not trust me, click the Tables group to view
   the names of tables in your database.

Importing the database table from another database

Rare things are more monotonous than entering records in a database table. In case the record you want was already imputed somewhere else, more power to you. Kindly follow these instructions to obtain a database table from another Access database:

1. **Visit the External data tab.**

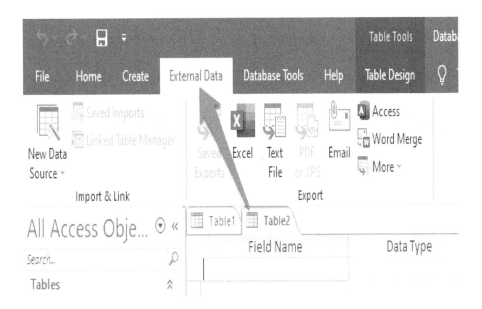

2. **Click the New Data Source button, and in the File Open dialog box, choose the Access database with the table you need and click Open.** The Get External Data-Access Database dialog box unlocks.

3. **Click the Browse Button, and in the File Open dialog box, choose the Access database with the table you need and click Open.** You go back to the Get External Data-Access Database dialog box.

4. **Choose the first option button (Import Tables, Queries, Forms, Reports, Macros, and Modules into the Recent Database) and then click OK.**

5. **Choose the database table you want on the Tables tab.** You can import more than one database table by clicking the Select All button or clicking numerous table names.

6. **Then click OK.**

Obtaining the help of a template

Kindly follow these steps to obtain the help of a template in creating a table (and accompanying queries, reports, and forms):

1. **Close all objects in case any objects are open.** To close an object, click its Close button or right-click its tab and select Close on the shortcut menu.

2. **Click the Application Parts button on the Create tab.** A drop-down menu with options for creating forms and tables comes into sight. (The tables are listed under 'Quick Start').

3. **Select Contacts, Issues, Tasks, or Users.** In case you have other tables in your database, a dialog box asks you if you want to create a relationship between the table you are creating and another table.

4. **Choose the There Is No Relationship option button and click Create.** "Establishing Relationships among Database Tables" explains how to create relationships on your own and this will be explained later in this chapter. But if you want to create these relationships now and you have the means to do it, choose an option besides There is No Relationship, select a table on the drop-down menu, and then click the Next button to select which field to forge the relationship with.

5. **On the Navigation pane, right-click the name of the table you created and select Design View.** In the Design view, you can view the names of the fields in the table.

Opening and Viewing Tables

To unlock a table, start in the Navigation pane and choose the Tables group to see the names of the database tables you created. The way you unlock a table depends on whether you want to open it in the Design view or Datasheet view.

❖ Design view is for creating fields and describing their parameters.

❖ Datasheet view is for entering and examining data in a table.

Pick a table on the Navigation pane and use one of these methods to open and view it:

- ❖ **Opening in Design View:** Right-click the table's name in the Navigation pane and select Design View on the shortcut menu.

- ❖ **Opening in Datasheet view:** On the Navigation pane, double-click the table's name or right-click its name and select Open on the shortcut menu.

- ❖ **Switching between views by right-clicking:** Right-click the table's tab and select Datasheet View or Design View.

- ❖ **Switching between views on the status bar:** click the Datasheet View or Design View button on the right side of the status bar.

- ❖ **Switching between views with the View button:** On the Home tab, click the View Button and select Datasheet View or Design View.

Entering and Changing Table Fields

The next thing to do after you have created a database table is to enter the fields, and if Access created the table for you, you just need to change the fields to your taste. Fields determine what kind of information is kept in a database table.

Generating a field

You can generate a field on your own or obtain Access's help and create a ready-made field. Both methods are discussed here.

Generating a field on your own

To generate a field on your own, unlock the table that needs a new field and follow the instructions on the (Table Tools) Table Design tab:

1. **Change to design view if you are not already there:** To change to Design view, click the Design View button on the status bar.

2. **Insert a new row for the field, if necessary:** To do this, click in the field that is to go after the new field, then click the insert Rows button on the (Table Tools) Table Design tab.

3. **Enter a name in the Field Name column:** Names can not be longer than 64 letters and they cannot include periods.

4. Press the Tab key or click in the Data Type column, and select a data type from the drop-down list, as displayed in the image below:

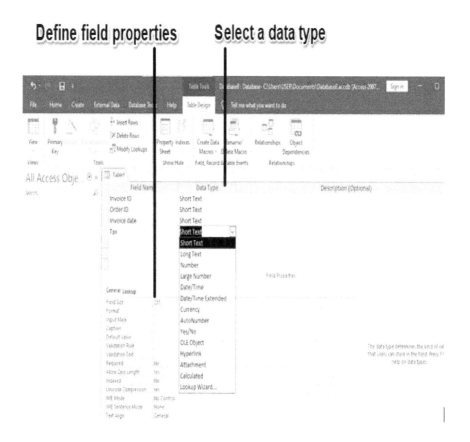

5. **Enter a description in the Description column this is optional:** These descriptions can be very useful when you want to reacquaint yourself with a field and discover what it is meant for.

Taking advantage of ready-made fields

To create a ready-made field, kindly follow the steps below:

❖ **Change to Datasheet view by clicking the datasheet view button.**

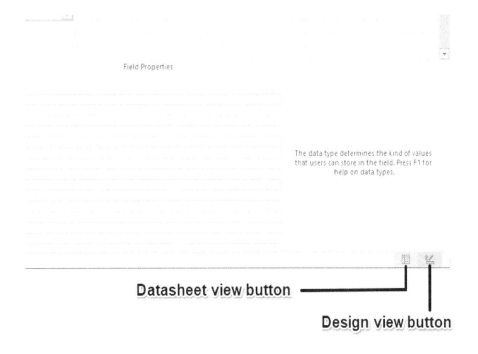

❖ **Choose the field that you want your recent field to go after.**

❖ **On the (Table Tools) Table Fields tab, click a field button or click the More Fields button and select the name of a field on the drop-down list.**

Search for field buttons in the Add & Delete group. Field buttons include Short Text, Currency, and Number. After you create your recent field, change to Design view and examine its field properties. Some of these properties may require changing. See "Field Properties for Making Sure That Data Entries Are Accurate" for information concerning field properties.

Everything about data types

Data types are the first line of defense in making sure that data is imputed accurately in a table, to select a data type for a field, start in Design view, unlock the Data Type drop-down menu, and select a data type. Select data types carefully, because the way you classify the data that is imputed in a field determines how you query the field for information. The table below discusses the options on the Data Type drop-down list.

Data Types for Fields

Data Type	What it is meant for
Short Text	For storing text (city names, for instance) combinations of text and numbers (street addresses, for instance) numbers that won't be calculated (telephone numbers, social security numbers, ZIP codes, for instance)
Long Text	For keeping long descriptions.
Number	For keeping numbers to be used in calculations or sorting.
Large Number	For importing and linking to Bright (big integer) data. This data type is for working with calculations involving extremely large numbers

Currency	For keeping monetary figures for use in calculating and storing.
Date/Time	For keeping dates and times and using dates and times in calculations.
Date/Time Extended	For keeping dates and times such that they are compatible with the SQL Server datatime2 data type.
Yes/No	For keeping True/False, Yes/No, and On/off type data.
AutoNumber	For imputing numbers in sequence that will be distinct from record to record. Use this data type for the primary key field.
OLE Object	This is used for embedding an OLE link in your Access table to another object Excel worksheet or Word document.
Calculated	For entering a mathematical expression that uses data from other fields in the database table.
Hyperlink	For keeping hyperlinks to other locations on the internet.
Lookup Wizard	For creating a drop-down list with choices that a data-entry clerk can select from when entering data.
Attachment	This is used for keeping an image, spreadsheet, document, chart, or other file.

Designating the primary key field

Selecting a primary key field is so essential that Access does not let you close a table unless you select one. Follow these instructions on the (Table Tools) Table Design tab to designate a field in a database table as the primary key field:

177

- ❖ **In Design view, choose the field or fields you want to be the primary key:** To choose a field, click its row selector, the slight box by its left; Ctrl+click row selectors to choose more than one field.
- ❖ **Click the Primary Key button:** A slight key symbol displays on the row selector to let you know which field or fields are the primary key fields.

To remove a primary key, click its row selector and then click the Primary Key button all over again.

Moving, renaming, and deleting fields

To move, rename, or delete a field. Change to Design view and kindly follow these steps:

- ❖ **Moving a field:** Choose the field's row selector and release the mouse button. Then click one more time and drag the selector up or down to a new location.
- ❖ **Renaming a field:** Click in the Field Name box where the name is, delete the name that is there, and enter a new name.
- ❖ **Deleting a field:** Click in the Field Name box, visit the (Table Tools) Table Design tab, and click the Delete Rows button. You can also right-click the field and select Delete Rows on the shortcut menu.

CHAPTER THREE

Field Properties for Making Sure That Data Entries Are Precise

People do make mistakes when they enter data in a database table. One way to cut down on mistakes is to take advantage of the Field Properties settings on the General tab in the Design view window.

Field properties | **Description of the property**

Field Properties

General Lookup
Field Size
Format
Input Mask
Caption
Default Value
Validation Rule
Validation Text
Required   No
Allow Zero Length   Yes
Indexed   No
Unicode Compression   Yes
IME Mode   No Control
IME Sentence Mode   None
Text Align   General

The maximum number of characters you can enter in the field. The largest maximum you can set is 255. Press F1 for help on field size.

Field Properties settings

The field properties settings safeguard data from being entered wrongly. Following is a description of the diverse properties and a guide for using them wisely.

Field Size

In the Field Size box for Text Fields, input the maximum number of characters that can be entered in the field. For instance, if the field you are dealing with is a ZIP code, and you need to input six-number ZIP codes. By inputting 6 in the Field Size text box, only six characters can be entered in the field. A sleepy data-entry clerk could not enter a seven-character ZIP code by coincidence.

Format

This has been discussed earlier in this chapter. Click the drop-down list and select the format in which text, numbers, dates, and times are shown.

Decimal Places

For a field that grasps numbers, unlock the Decimal Places drop-down menu and select how many numbers can appear to the right of the decimal point.

Input Mask

This feature offers a template with punctuation marks to make entering the data easier, for Text and Date field types. Social security numbers, Telephone numbers, and other numbers that typically are entered along with dashes and parentheses are ideal candidates for an input mask.

Caption

In case the field you are working on has a cryptic or difficult-to-understand name, impute a more descriptive name in the Caption text box.

Value Default

When you notice that the majority of records require a certain value, number, or abbreviation, enter it in the Default Value text box.

Validation Rule

When you can find your way around operators and Boolean expressions, you can establish a rule for entering data in a field. For instance, you can impute an expression that requires dates to be imputed in a certain time frame. Below are some examples of validation rules:

<800	The value you enter must be less than 800
>800	The value you enter must be above 800
<>0	The value you enter cannot be zero
>=#1/1/2024#	The date you enter must be January 1, 2024, or later.

Validation Text

If someone imputes data that disrupts a validation rule that you impute in the validation Rule text box, Access shows a standard error message.

Required

By evasion, no entry has to be made in a field, but if you select Yes instead of No in the Required box and you fail to make an entry in the field, a message box informs you to be sure to make an entry.

Allow Zero Length

This property permits you to enter zero-length strings in a field. A zero-length string which is indicated by two quotation marks with no text or spaces between them ("") –reveals that no value exists for a field.

Indexed

This property shows whether the field has been indexed. As "Indexing for Faster Sorts, Searches, and Queries" clarifies, later in this chapter, indexes make sorting fields and searching through a field go faster.

Unicode Expression

Select Yes from the Unicode Expression drop-down list if you want to compress data that is now kept in Unicode format, which is a standardized encoding scheme. When you store data in this manner it saves on disk space, and you perhaps don't want to change this property.

Smart Tags

If you want to enter Smart Tags in the field, specify which kind you enter by clicking the three dots next to the Smart Tags box and selecting an option in the Action Tags dialog box.

Text Align

This property regulates how the text is aligned in a column or on a report or form. pick General to let Access determine the alignment, or choose Left, Right, Center, or distribute.

Text Format

This drop-down list lets you select to permit rich text in the field, It is obtainable on the Long Text field. With this property set to Rich Text, you can make diverse words bold, italic, underline, and modify font sizes and colors. Set it to Plain Text for plain, boring text with no formatting.

Append Only

This property lets you add data only to a Long Text field to collect a history of comments, it is obtainable on Long Text fields.

Show Date Picker

This property is obtainable on the Date/Time fields. Select Dates to place a button next to the column that data-entry clerks can click to open a calendar and choose a date instead of typing numbers.

IME Mode/IME Sentence mode

These options are for changing characters and sentences from East Asian versions of Access.

Creating a lookup data-entry list

Conceivably the best way to make sure that data is imputed accurately is to create a data-entry drop-down list. Therefore, anybody entering the data in your database table can do so by selecting an item from the list and not by typing it in, this technique saves time and prevents invalid data from being entered. Access provides two ways to create the drop-down list:

❖ **Create the list by entering the items yourself:** You can take this path when you are dealing with a finite list of items that never change.

❖ **Obtain the items from another database table:** Take this path to get items from a column in another database table. In this manner, you can select from an ever-expanding list of items. This is an amazing way of getting items from a primary key field in another table. When the number of items in the other database changes, so as well the number of items in the drop-down list, because the items come from the other database table.

Creating a drop-down list on your own

Kindly follow these instructions to create a drop-down, or lookup, list with entries you type:

1. **Pick the field that requires a drop-down list, in Design view.**

2. **Unlock the Data Type drop-down list and select Lookup Wizard, the last option in the list.**

   The Lookup Wizard dialog box comes into sight.

3. **Choose the second option, I will type in the Data that I desire, and then click the Next button.**

4. **Underneath Col 1 in the next dialog box, enter each item you want to appear in the drop-down list; then click the Next button.**

   You can generate a multicolumn list by entering a number in the Number of Columns text box and then entering items for the list.

5. **Enter a name for the field, if essential, and click the finish button.**

   Navigate to Datasheet view and unlock the drop-down list in the field to make sure that it shows appropriately.

To eliminate a lookup list from a field, choose the field, visit the Lookup tab in the Design view window, unlock the Display Control drop-down list, and select Text Box. See the Lookup properties in the image below:

Getting list items from a database table

Follow these instructions below to get items in a drop-down list from another database table:

1. **In Design view, click the field that wants a list, unlock the Data Type drop-down list, and select Lookup Wizard.**

    The Lookup Wizard dialog box appears.

2. **Choose the first option, I want the Lookup Field to Get the Values from Another Query or Table. Then click Next.**

    You notice a list of tables in your database.

3. **Choose the table with the data you want and click the Next button.**

    The dialog box displays a list of obtainable fields in the table.

4. **Choose the field where the data for your list is kept.**
5. **Click the > button.**
    The names of the lists are displayed on the right-hand side of the dialog box, under Selected Fields.

6. **Click the Next button.**
7. **Then click the Finish button.**

Indexing for Faster Sorts, Searches, and Queries

In a large database table, indexes make sorting, searching, and querying go greatly faster because Access looks through its data rather than the data in tables. Indexing means to instruct Access to keep information about the data in a field or combination of fields.

Indexing a field

To index a field, change to Design view, choose the field you want to index, and on the General tab of the field Properties part of the Design window, unlock the indexed drop-down list and select one of these options:

➤ **Yes (Duplicates OK):** Indexes the field and permits duplicate values to be entered in the field.

➤ **Yes (No Duplicates):** Indexes the field and disallows duplicate values.

Indexing created on more than one field

An index generated on more than one field is known as a multifield index. Multifield indexes make sorting, searching, and querying the database table go faster. Kindly follow the steps below to generate a multifield index:

➤ **Change to Design view, and on the (Table Tools) Table Design tab, click the indexes button.**

You notice the indexes dialog box, as displayed in the image below.

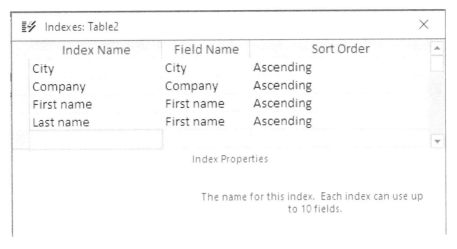

> ➢ On the blank line in the dialog box, impute a name for the index in the index Name column.
> ➢ Unlock the drop-down list and select the first field you want for the multifield index.

Access sorts the records first on this field and then on the second field you select.

> **In the next row, leave the index Name blank and select another field name from the drop-down menu.**

This field is the second field in the index. You can use as many as ten diverse fields in a multifield index.

> **Select Descending in the Sort Order column in case you want the field sorted in descending order.**

Whenever you want to leave the Sort Order set to Ascending because most people read from A to Z.

> **Click the Close button.**

Dealing with tables in the Relationships window

Unlock the Relationship window to manage database tables and their relationships to each other. To unlock this window, visit the Database Tools tab and click the Relationships button. Access unlocks the (Relationship Tools) Relationship Design tab for you to deal with table relationships.

Before you can create a relationship between tables, you have to position tables in the Relationships Design window. Kindly follow these instructions to add a table to the window:

> **In the (Relationships Tools) Relationships Design tab, select the Add Tables button (You may have to click the Database Tool first).**

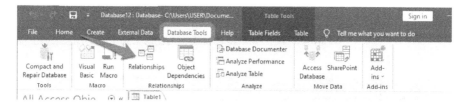

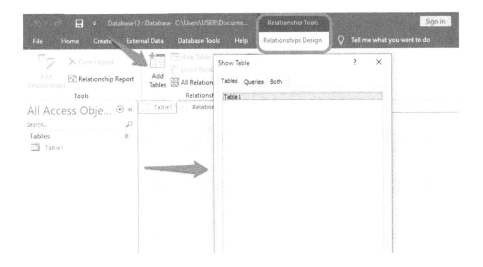

> **Drag a table name from the task pane into the window.**

Falsifying relationships between tables

On the (Relationship Tools) Relationships Design tab, then be certain that both tables are on display and kindly follow these instructions to falsify a relationship between them:

1. **Click to choose the field in one table; then grasp down the mouse button, drag the pointer to the field in the other table where you need to falsify the link, and then release the mouse button.**
2. **Choose the Enforce Referential Integrity check box:** if you do not choose this box, the relationship between the tables is unclassified, instead of being a one-to-many relationship.
3. **Choose Cascade options if you so select.**

   One of these options is amazing; the other is hazardous:

> **Cascade Update Related Fields:** in case you change a value on the "one" side of the relationship, a matching value on the "many" side changes as well to preserve referential honesty.

➢ **Cascade Delete Related Records:** if you delete a record in the "one" table, all records in the "many" table to which the deleted record is linked are also deleted.

4. **Click the Create button to falsify the relationship.**

Editing and Deleting table relationships

In the Relationships window, choose the line that signifies the relationship between two database tables and follow these steps to edit or remove the relationship:

❖ **Editing the relationship:** Click the Edit Relationships button, right-click and select Edit Relationships, or double-click the line. The relationship dialog box appears, where you can refit the relationship.

❖ **Deleting the relationship:** Press the Delete key or right-click and select Delete. Then choose Yes in the confirmation box.

CHAPTER FOUR

Entering the Data

Finally, you can now start entering the data. If you have set up your database tables, named your fields, and established relationships between the tables, you are good to go. This chapter describes how to enter the data in a database table it also explains how to find missing records in case one goes off track.

Two Ways to Enter Data

There are two ways to enter data in a database table, they are Database view and a form. here are the benefits of entering data in the Datasheet view:

- ❖ You can compare data easily between records.
- ❖ You can navigate up or down to find records.
- ❖ Many records appear simultaneously.
- ❖ You can sort by column with the commands in the Sort and Filter group on the Home tab.

Below are the advantages of entering the data in a form:

- ❖ Getting from field to field is easier.
- ❖ Fields are clearly labeled so that you always see what to enter.
- ❖ You don't have to navigate left or right to view all the fields.

Entering the Data in Datasheet View

In Datasheet view, the bottommost of the window states how many records are entered in the database table and which record the cursor is in. To enter a new record, go to a new, empty row and begin to enter the data. To create a new row, kindly do one of the following:

- ❖ **On the Home tab, click the New button.**
- ❖ **Click the New (Blank) Record button in the Datasheet navigation buttons.** These buttons can be found beneath the left corner of the Datasheet view window.
- ❖ **Navigate to the bottommost of the Datasheet view window and begin typing in the row with an asterisk (*) next to it.**
- ❖ **Press Ctrl++(the plus key).**

A pencil icon comes into sight on the row selector to let you discover which record you are working with. To navigate from field to field, click in a field, press enter, or press the Tab key.

To delete a record, click its row selector and press the delete key or the Delete button (which can be found on the Home Tab).

Two tricks for entering data quicker

In a database with numerous fields, sometimes it's difficult to tell what data to enter. When the pointer is in the sixth or seventh field, for instance, you can lose sight of the first field, the one on the left side of the datasheet that usually identifies the person or item whose record you are entering.

To freeze a field so that it displays onscreen no matter how you navigate to the right side of the datasheet, right-click the field's column heading and select Freeze Fields on the shortcut menu. To unfreeze the fields, right-click the column heading and select Unfreeze All Fields on the shortcut menu. You can also freeze more than one field by dragging over field names at the topmost of the datasheet before selecting to freeze the columns.

Another way to deal with the issue of not being able to recognize where data is supposed to be entered is to hide columns in the datasheet. To execute this trick, kindly follow the steps below:

> - **Choose the columns you want to hide by dragging the pointer across their names.**
> - **Right-click the column heading and select Hide Fields on the shortcut menu.**
> - **To view the columns one more time, right-click any column heading and select Unhide Fields on the shortcut menu.** The Unhide Columns dialog box appears.
> - **Choose the fields that you want to see on the datasheet.**

Entering the Data in a form

Forms like the one displayed below are easier for entering data. The label shows you exactly what to impute.

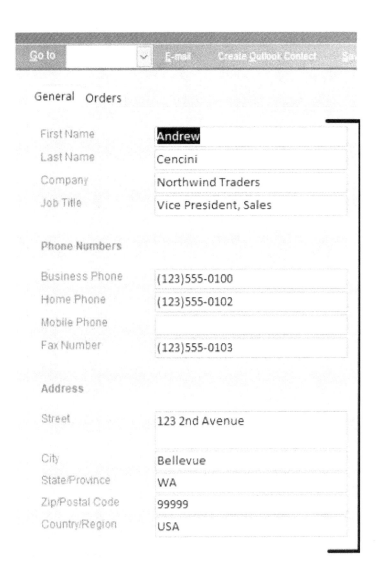

Creating a form

To create a form, visit the Create tab and click the Form Wizard button.

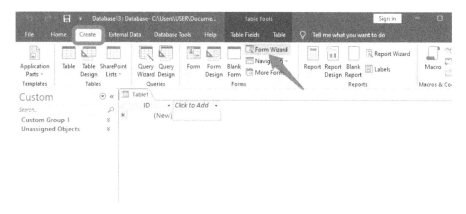

You will see the first of several Form Wizard dialog boxes. Provide an answer to these questions and continue clicking the Next button until the time comes to click Finish:

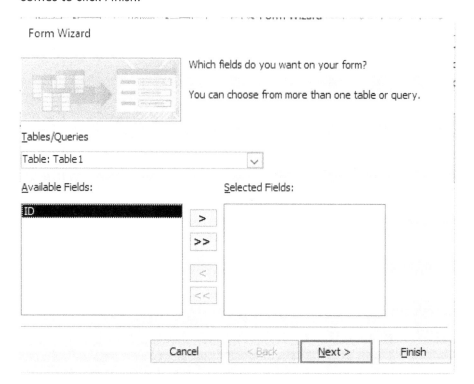

- ❖ **Tables/Queries:** From the drop-down menu, select the name of the database table you want to enter data in.
- ❖ **Selected Fields:** Click the >>button to enter all the field names in the Select Fields box.

- ❖ **Layout:** Choose the Columnar option button. The other layouts are not very decent for entering data in a table. If you select Datasheet or Tabular. You can also enter data straight into the datasheet instead of depending on a form.
- ❖ **Title:** Give your form a name after the table you created it in other to recognize it easily in the Navigation pane.

To delete a form, right-click its name in the Navigation pane and select Delete on the shortcut menu.

Entering the data

If you want to unlock a form and start entering data in its database table, show the form's name in the Navigation pane and double-click the form's name. you can also right-click the form and select Open.

To enter data in a form, click the New (Blank) Record button. this button can be found with the Navigation buttons at the base of the form window. A new, empty form displays. Begin typing. Press the Tab key, press the Enter key, or click to navigate from field to field. You can go backward through the fields by pressing Shift+Tab. If you enter the record to some level and you want to start from the beginning, press the Esc key to blank the recent field. Press Esc again to blank all the fields.

Discovery of a Missing Record

Sometimes you might not be able to locate the item or record you need so badly. In case this happens to you, Access provides the Find command. Unlock the database table with the data that requires finding. If you know the field in which the data is positioned, click on the field. Then, on the Home tab, click the Find button.

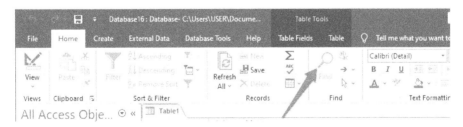

195

The Find and Replace dialog box appears. See the image below:

Fill in the dialog box as follows:

- ❖ **Find What:** Enter the item you are looking for in this box.
- ❖ **Look In:** if you click in a field before selecting the Find command, the Resent Field is chosen in this box. Select Current Document on the drop-down menu, to search the whole database table.
- ❖ **Search:** Select an option- All, UP, or Down- that explains the direction to start searching.
- ❖ **Match:** select the option that explains what you know about the item.
- ❖ **Match Case:** choose this check box, if you know the combination of lower and uppercase letters you are after and you enter the combination in the Find What text box.
- ❖ **Search Fields As Formatted:** select this check box if you are searching for a field that has been formatted a particular way, be certain that the number or text you imputed in the Find What text box is formatted appropriately.

Finding and Replacing Data

Finding and replacing data is unusually similar to finding data. The alteration is that you enter data in the Replace With text box as well as the acquainted Find What text box and other option boxes. To find and replace data, kindly follow the steps below:

- ❖ Visit the Home tab and click the Replace button
- ❖ After you enter the replacement data in the Replace With text box make sure that the entire Field is chosen in the Match drop-down menu.
- ❖ Conducting a find and replace operation with Any Part of the Field or Start of the Field selected in the Match drop-down menu can have unintended consequences.

CHAPTER FIVE

Sorting and Filtering for Data

Now that you have laid the foundation, you can put your database through its paces and make it do what databases are meant to do: offer information of one kind or another. This chapter describes how to beleaguer an Access database for names, dates, addresses, statistical averages, and so on. It reveals how to sort records and filter a database table to view records of a certain kind.

Sorting Records in a Database Table

For records to appear in alphabetical, numerical, or date order in one field, you need to sort the records in a database table. You can locate records faster by sorting them in a database. Records can be sorted in ascending or descending order.

Sorting records

Kindly follow the instructions below to sort records in a database table:

❖ **In Datasheet view, click anywhere in the field by which you want to sort the records.**

❖ **Click the Ascending or Descending button, on the Home tab.**

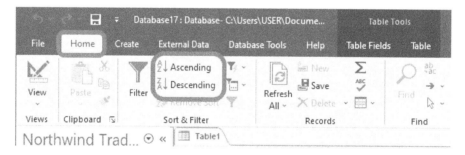

Filtering to discover information

Filtering isolates all the records in a database table that have the same field values or almost the same field values. For all the records in the table to be displayed on the datasheet, only records that meet the filtering criteria are displayed. The fundamental idea behind filtering is to select a field value in the database table and make use of it as the standard for locating or excluding records. For instance, you can find all the orders taken in June or all the orders for a particular customer.

Diverse ways to filter a database table

Below are the four ways to filter a database table. You have to visit the Datasheet view on the Home tab to start filtering operations.

- ❖ **Filter by Selection:** Select all or aspects of a field in the database table, click the Selection button, and select a filtering option. Access isolates all records with the data you choose.
- ❖ **Filter by Form:** Click the Advanced button and select Filter by Form. A form appears with one drop-down menu for each field in your table. From the drop-down menu, make selections to define the records you are searching for and click the Toggle Filter button.
- ❖ **Filter for Input:** Choose the field you want to filter with and click the Filter button. A dialog comes into sight for you to select values in the field.
- ❖ **Advanced Filter/Sort:** Click the Advanced button and select Advanced Filter/Sort. The Filter window unlocks. Drag the name of the field you want to filter into the grid. Then select a Sort option and enter a search criterion.

Unfiltering a database table

When you are done filtering a database table, apply one of these methods to unfilter it and view all the records in the table again:

- ❖ Click the word Filtered at the bottom of the window. You can click this word again or click the Toggle Filter button to repeat the filter operation.
- ❖ On the Home tab, click the Toggle Filter button, you can click this button again to repeat the filter operation.
- ❖ On the Home tab, click the Advanced button and select Clear All Filters on the drop-down menu.

Filtering by selection

Follow these instructions to filter by selection:

1. **Show the database table that requires filtering in the Datasheet view.**
2. **Inform Access how to filter the records:** to locate all records with the same text or value in a certain field, click in a field with the value or text.
3. **On the Home tab, click the Selection button and select a filtering option.**

Filtering by form

Kindly follow the steps below to filter by form:

1. **In Datasheet view, visit the Home tab, click the Advanced button, and then select Filter by form on the drop-down menu.**

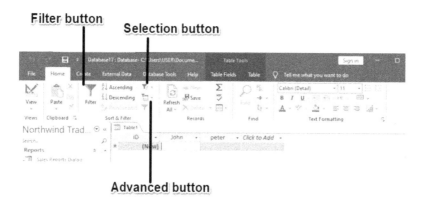

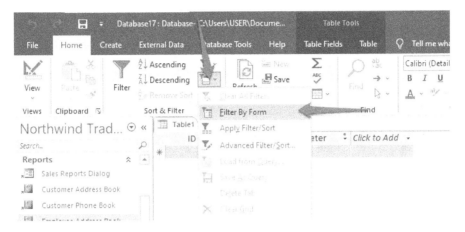

2. **Click in a field, unluck its drop-down menu, and select a value on the drop-down menu or enter a comparison value.**

3. **If you wish, enter more criteria for the filtering operation:** you can impute values in other fields and also filter more than once in the same field.

4. **Click the Toggle Filter button:** The outcomes of the filtering operation are displayed in the datasheet.

Filtering for input

Apply this method to detach records that fall within a numerical or date range. Kindly follow these instructions to filter for input:

1. **Show the database table that you want to filter in Datasheet view.**

2. **Choose the field with the data you want to use for the filter operation:** to choose a field, click its name along the top of the datasheet.

3. **On the Home tab, click the Filter button.**

4. **Inform Access how to filter the database table:** you can select values or describe a data range.

CHAPTER SIX

Querying: The fundamentals

Querying is all about asking questions of a database and obtaining an answer in the form of records that meet the query criteria. You need to query when you want to ask a thorough question of a database. Access provides numerous diverse ways to query a database which will be discussed later in this chapter. The following pages introduce you to queries, how to create them, and how to change them.

Creating a new query

To create a new query, begin on the Create tab and click the Query Wizard button or Query Design.

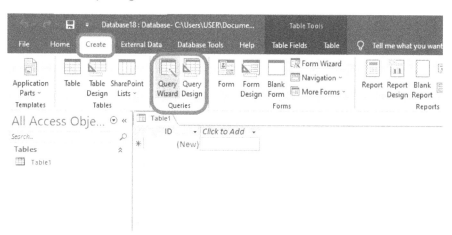

❖ **Create the query with a wizard:** Click the Query Wizard button to reveal the New Query dialog box select a wizard option and answer the questions that the Query Wizard asks.

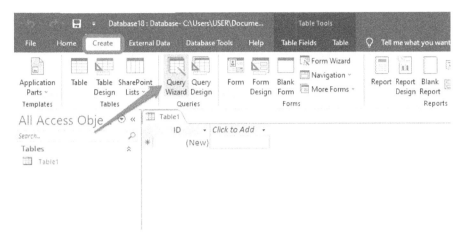

❖ **Create the query in Design view:** Click the Query Design button to view the Query in the Design window, then construct your query in the Design window.

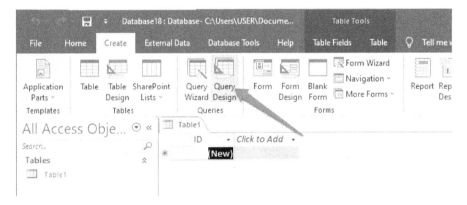

Viewing queries in Design and Datasheet views

Choose a query on the Navigation pane and apply these methods to view it in Datasheet or Design view. The datasheet view displays the outcomes of running a query. Create and change queries in the Design view.

➢ **Opening in Datasheet view:** On the Navigation pane, double-click the query's name and select Open on the shortcut menu.
➢ **Opening in Design view:** Right-click the query's name in the Navigation pane and select Design view on the shortcut menu.

Table pane

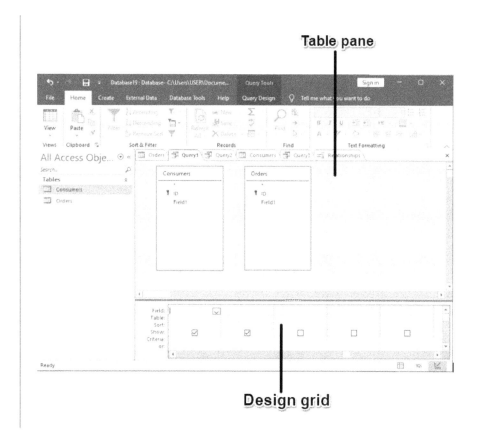

Design grid

> **Swapping between views on the status bar:** Click the Datasheet View or Design View button on the right-hand side of the status bar.
> **Swapping between views by right-clicking:** Right-click the query's title bar and select Datasheet View or Design View.
> **Swapping between views with the view button:** On the Home tab, unlock the drop-down list on the View button. then select Design View or Datasheet View on the drop-down list.

Navigating your way around the Query Design window

The Query Design window is where you create a query or retool a query you created already. Change to Design view to see the Query Design window. This window will appear immediately after you click the Query Design button to create a new query. The Query Design window is separated into halves:

> ➤ **Table pane:** Lists the database tables you are querying as well as the fields in each table. You can drag the tables to new locations or modify the size of the table by dragging it and seeing more fields.
> ➤ **Design grid:** Lists which fields to query from the tables, how to sort the query outcomes, which fields to display in the query results, and criteria for locating records in fields.

Selecting which database tables to query

Kindly follow the instructions below to select which database tables to obtain information from in a query:

❖ **Visit the (Query Tools) Query Design tab and click the Add Tables button.**

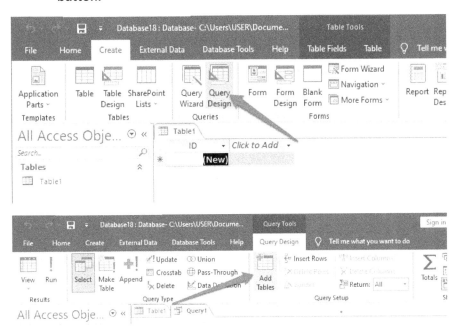

The Add Tables task pane unlocks. It lists all the tables in your database.

❖ **Position the names of tables you want to query in the Table pane**
You can apply these methods to position a table in the Table pane:
- Double-click a table name in the Add Tables task pane.
- Drag a table name from the Add Tables task pane to the Table pane.

- Ctrl+click table names to select more than one table, and then drag the table names onto the Table pane.

Click the Add Tables button on the (Query Tools) Query Design tab, If you cannot see the Add Tables task pane.

Selecting which fields to query

Immediately after you have selected which tables to query, the next thing to do is to select which fields to query from the tables you chose. The object is to list fields from the Table pane in the first row of the Design grid. Data from fields listed in the first row of the Design grid is used to produce query results.

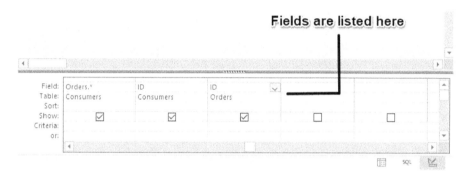

Access provides these methods for listing field names in the first row of the Design grid:

- ❖ **Dragging a field name:** Drag a field name into a column on the Design grid.
- ❖ **Double-clicking a field name:** double-click a field name to position it in the next available column in the Design grid.
- ❖ **Selecting a table and field name:** click in the Table row, unlock the drop-down menu, and select the name of a table. Then in the Field box directly above, unlock the drop-down menu and select a field name.
- ❖ **Choosing all the fields in a table:** In the case you want all the fields from a table to display in the query outcomes, either double-click the asterisk(*) at the top of the list of the field names or drag the asterisk into the Design grid.

206

If you want to remove a field name from the Design grid, choose it and press the Delete key or visit the (Query Tools) Query Design tab and click the Delete Columns button.

Sorting the query outcomes or results

The sorted row of the Design grid below the Table name entails a drop-down menu. To sort the query, click the drop-down menu in a field and select Ascending or Descending to sort the results of a query on a certain field. To sort the outcomes or results on many fields, be certain that the first field to be sorted displays to the left of the other fields. Access reads the sort order from left to right.

MOVING FIELD COLUMNS ON THE QUERY GRID

Kindly follow these instructions to put field columns in the right order in the Query grid:

1. **Click a column's selector button to choose a column.**

   This button is the narrow gray box directly above the field name.

2. **Click the selector button again and drag the column to the left or right.**

Entering criteria for a query

What distinguishes a run-of-the-mill query from a supercharged query is a criterion, an expression you enter on the Criteria line beneath a field. Enter criteria on the Criteria line of the Query grid. By entering criteria, you can locate records in the database with amazing correctness.

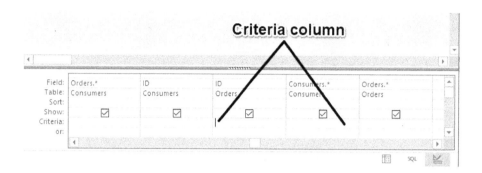

Criteria column

Field:	Orders.*	ID	ID	Consumers.*	Orders.*
Table:	Consumers	Consumers	Orders	Consumers	Orders
Sort:					
Show:	☑	☑	☑	☑	☑
Criteria:					
or:					

When you need assistance writing an expression for a query, try clicking the Builder button to create your query in the Expression Builder dialog box. This button can be found on the (Query Tools) Query Design tab. Some of the Criteria to enter are listed below:

- Numeric criteria
- Text criteria
- Date criteria

Saving and running a query

To save a query and engrave its name forever in the Navigation pane, click the Save button on the Quick Access toolbar and enter a descriptive name in the Save As dialog box. The name you enter displays in the Queries group in the Navigation pane.

After you strenuously create your query, take it for a test drive. To run a query:

- ➢ **Starting from the Query Design window:** Click the Run button on the (Query Tools) Design tab.
- ➢ **Starting from the Navigation pane:** Double-click an existing query's name, and select Open on the shortcut menu.

Six kinds of Queries

Access provides a numerous kind of queries but I will only be explaining six of them in this chapter:

- ❖ **Select Query:** A select query is the standard kind of query, which I discussed earlier in this chapter. It puts together information from one or more database tables and shows the information in a datasheet. It is the most common query and the starting point for most other queries.
- ❖ **Top-value query:** A top-value query is an easy way to locate, in a Number or Currency field, the lowest or highest values.
- ❖ **Summary query:** This is the same as a top-value query, it is a way of obtaining collective information about all the data in a field.
- ❖ **Calculation query:** A calculation query is one in which calculations are performed as an aspect of the query. Follow the steps below to create a calculation query:
    - Create a query as you always do and be certain to include the fields you want to use for calculation purposes in the Query grid.

    - Impute a name for the Calculation field and follow it with a colon, in the Field box of a blank field.

    - After the colon, in square brackets ([]), impute the name of a field whose data you use for the calculation.

    - Complete the calculation.

    - Click the Run button to run your calculation query.

- ❖ **Update query:** An update query is a way to reach into a database and update records in numerous diverse tables all at a time. Kindly follow the steps below to run an Update query:

- Visit the Design view, move to the (Query Tools) Query Design tab, and click the Update button.

- In the field with data that requires updating, impute text or a value in the Update To line.

- Click the Run button.

❖ **Delete Query:** A delete query deletes records and does not give you the privilege to obtain the records back if you change your mind about deleting them. Be careful about running delete queries.

CHAPTER SEVEN

Presenting Data in a Report

The best way to present data in a database table or query is to present it in a report. Reports are easy to read and understand. In this chapter, you will learn how to create reports, open them, and edit them.

Creating a Report

The most appropriate way to create a report is to base your report on a query. You can query your database from inside the Report Wizard. The best way is to run a query to produce the results you want in your report, save your query, and then create a report from the query results. How to create a query has been explained in chapter six of this mini-book.

To create a report with the Report Wizard, visit the Create tab and click the Report Wizard button. you notice the first of numerous Report Wizard dialog boxes. Consult the dialog boxes as follows, clicking the Next button as you move along:

- ❖ **Tables/Queries:** Unlock the Table/Queries drop-down menu and select the query where the information in the report will come from. A list of fields in the query is displayed in the Available Field box.
- ❖ **Available Fields and Selected Fields:** Choose the fields whose data you want in the report by choosing the fields one at a time and clicking the >button. by doing this, it moves field names from the Available Fields box to the Selected Fields box. Add all the field names by clicking the >>button.
- ❖ **Do you want to Add Any Grouping Levels?** Add subheadings in your report by selecting a field name and clicking the >button to make it a subheading.
- ❖ **What Sort of Order Do You Want?** Choose up to four fields to sort the data in your report.
- ❖ **How would you like to lay your report?** To select a layout for your report, experiment with the options, and see the Preview box. You may have to print your report in Landscape View if your report has a lot of fields.

❖ **What Title Do You Want for Your Report?** Enter a descriptive title. The name you select displays in the Reports group in the Navigation pane.

❖ **Preview the Report:** Pick this option button and click Finish.

Below is an example image of a Report.

				Monday, March 11, 2024

Top 10 Biggest Orders

	Invoice #	Order Date	Company	Sales Amount
1	38	3/10/2006	Company BB	$13,800.00
2	41	3/24/2006	Company G	$13,800.00
3	47	4/8/2006	Company F	$4,200.00
4	46	4/5/2006	Company I	$3,690.00
5	58	4/22/2006	Company D	$3,520.00
6	79	6/23/2006	Company F	$2,490.00
7	77	6/5/2006	Company Z	$2,250.00
8	36	2/23/2006	Company C	$1,930.00
9	44	3/24/2006	Company A	$1,674.75
10	78	6/5/2006	Company CC	$1,560.00

Opening and Viewing Reports

Kindly follow the steps below to open a report:

1. **In the Navigation pane, choose the Reports group.**

   You will notice the names of the reports you created.

2. **Double-click a report name or right-click a name and select Open from the shortcut menu.**

   The report is displayed in Report view.

Fine-tuning a Report

Access provides numerous tools for modifying the layout and appearance of a report. In the Report group of the Navigation pane, right-click a report and select Layout View on the shortcut menu. Your report comes into sight in Layout view, as displayed below, in this view, using tools on the (Report Layout Tools) Report Layout Design, Arrange, Format, and Page Setup tabs, you can fine-tune your report's appearance.

You can modify a report's appearance in Report Layout View without navigating too much trouble if you kindly follow these steps:

❖ **Selecting a new layout:** On the (Report Layout Tools) Arrange tab, click the Tabular button and select an option on the drop-down menu, to modify your report's layout.

❖ **Including page numbers:** Visit the (Report Layout Tools) Report Layout Design tab and click the Page Numbers button.

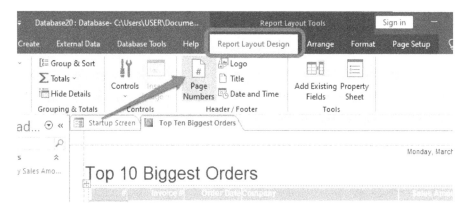

The Page Number dialog box appears, see the image below:

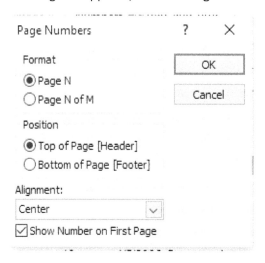

Select the Page N option to show a page number only, or choose the Page N of M option button to show a page number as well as the total number of pages in the report. Select Position and Alignment options to clarify where on the page to place the page number.

❖ **Changing the margins:** On the (Report Layout Tools) Page Setup tab, click the Margins button and pick Normal, Wide, or Narrow on the drop-down l

CONCLUSION

I believe you now have in-depth knowledge of how to use Microsoft Publisher after going through every aspect of this book, I am very sure you can now Start Publisher and navigate your way around the ribbon tab, and I also believe you now know how to layout and design your page, use text boxes, borders, accents, and page parts, use pre-design templates, build your template, format text such as bold, underlined, italic, and strike, to learn about typography, align text, highlight text, and also change text color, copy, paste, cut, and make use of the clipboard, add photos, crop, wrap text, use effects, save your publication, convert your publications to other formats, and also how to print your publications.

I also believe you now have in-depth knowledge of how to use Microsoft Access 365 after going through every aspect of this book, I am very sure you can now Start Access and navigate your way around the ribbon tab, and I also believe you now know how to Create a database file that you will use to save the database information, and also working with the Access Navigation pane, construction of the database table, Entering fields into each database table, Entering data directly into the table or employ the help of a Form, and many more.

INDEX

Access 365, 5
addresses, 193
Adjusting Font Size, 21
Adjusting Your Images, 69
Advertisements, 89
Alignment, 40, 78
Altering Text Boxes, 35
Ascending, 202
asterisk, 201
blueprint, 88
bold, 178
Booklets, 122
Borders, 33
Borders and Accents, 86
Calculation query, 204
Caption, 63
Cell Border, 51
clipart, 59
clipboard, 210
Close button, 165
columns, 43
confirmation box., 185
Criteria, 202
Cropping Images, 64
custom margins', 39
database, 142
database table, 160, 174
Datasheet View, 167
defense, 171
descriptive name, 176
Design grid, 200
Design view, 166
Design window, 183
dialog box, 163
dialog boxes, 99
displayed, 182
displays, 180
Drop Cap Features, 26
entering, 145
entering data, 187
equivalent, 144
Field Size, 175
field value, 193
Fields box, 189

File Backstage, 12
filtering, 195
Find button., 190
fine-tune, 208
Formatting, 45
General tab, 181
hazardous, 184
history, 178
home ribbon, 23
image thumbnail, 58
information, 171
Inserting a Row, 46
instructions, 164
irreplaceable, 142
Landscape, 206
Layout View, 208
Ligatures, 28
Lookup, 179
Mail Marge, 97
mailings, 102
Managing Publication, 112
Margins, 14
Match Case, 191
Merge cells, 48
Microsoft Access, 4
Microsoft Publisher, 6
navigation pane, 129
Navigation pane, 163
Numeric criteria, 203
Object Layers, 82
Objects Distribution, 79
opening screen, 151
outcomes, 198
Page Design Tab, 11
Page Masters, 125
Page parts, 82
placeholders., 83
Pre-designed, 108
property, 177
Publication, 73
Publication Size, 14
query, 146, 197
Query dialog box, 197
Report Wizard, 206

Reports, 206
review results', 101
Shadow, 76
Shadows, 30
shortcut menu, 187
simultaneously, 186
single sheet, 134
sorted, 193
Specifying Font, 20
Specifying Text Alignment, 23
status bar., 199
Summary query, 204
table names, 165
Table pane, 201
Tabular., 190
technique, 178
template, 151
Templates, 108
Text Autofit, 38
Text Direction, 37, 54

Text Effects, 29
text, numbers, dates, 175
The address book, 143
The building blocks, 160
The Main Workspace, 16
the relationship, 166
The Ribbon Tabs, 9
the row selector, 187
Toggle Filter button, 194
Typography Features, 25
Update query, 204
Using Page Setup, 119
validation rules, 176
Wizard, 179
Wizard button, 188
WordArt, 91
WordArt styles, 31
Working Graphics, 55
WORKING WITH GUIDES, 17
Wrapping Text, 70